The Anatomy of Resource Wars

MICHAEL RENNER

Thomas Prugh, *Editor*

WORLDWATCH PAPER 162

October 2002

FINANCIAL SUPPORT for the Institute is provided by the Ford Foundation, the Richard & Rhoda Goldman Fund, the George Gund Foundation, the William and Flora Hewlett Foundation, The Frances Lear Foundation, the Steve Leuthold Foundation, the Charles Stewart Mott Foundation, the Curtis and Edith Munson Foundation, the John D. and Catherine T. MacArthur Foundation, the Overbrook Foundation, the David and Lucile Packard Foundation, the Surdna Foundation, Inc., the Turner Foundation, Inc., UN Environment Programme, the Wallace Global Fund, the Weeden Foundation, and the Winslow Foundation. The Institute also receives financial support from its Council of Sponsors members—Adam and Rachel Albright, Tom and Cathy Crain, and Robert Wallace and Raisa Scriabine—and from the many other friends of Worldwatch.

THE WORLDWATCH PAPERS provide in-depth, quantitative, and qualitative analysis of the major issues affecting prospects for a sustainable society. The *Papers* are written by members of the Worldwatch Institute research staff and reviewed by experts in the field. They have been used as concise and authoritative references by governments, nongovernmental organizations, and educational institutions worldwide. For a partial list of available *Worldwatch Papers*, see back pages.

Table of Contents

Figures and Tables

ACKNOWLEDGEMENTS: A number of colleagues provided invaluable feedback on various drafts of this paper. Michael Ross of the University of California, Philippe Le Billon at the International Institute for Strategic Studies in London, and James Paul of the Global Policy Forum in New York City took time out from busy schedules to review the manuscript. I am also grateful to all of my Worldwatch research colleagues for their comments. In particular, I would like to thank David Roodman (now at the Center for Global Development) and Payal Sampat for their comments. And I am indebted to Uta Saoshiro, whose untiring research support and ready smile made a big difference. Special thanks are due to Tom Prugh for his steady hand in guiding the manuscript through the editing process, Lyle Rosbotham for his unique design abilities, and Richard Bell, Susan Finkelpearl, Susanne Martikke, and Leanne Mitchell for outreach help. Finally, my wife Annette and my children Paul and Judith have provided me with what is perhaps the most important element: a measure of balance between work and play.

MICHAEL RENNER joined the Institute in 1987. He is a Senior Researcher and serves as the Project Director for *Vital Signs*. His research deals with peace, security, and disarmament issues, and focuses in particular on the linkages among environment, natural resources, and violent conflict. Michael is the author of nine previous Worldwatch Papers, including *Ending Violent Conflict* (April 1999) and *Small Arms, Big Impact* (October 1997). His 1996 book *Fighting for Survival: Environmental Decline, Social Conflict, and the New Age of Insecurity* examined the ways in which resource scarcity can contribute to conflict.

The Relationship Between Resources and Conflict

Jonas Savimbi led a violent life and died a violent death. Yet when the leader of the Angolan rebel group UNITA (União Nacional para a Independência Total de Angola) was killed in an ambush in February 2002, his death freshened hopes that Angola might finally emerge from the nightmare of a quarter-century of nearly uninterrupted civil war. In short order, a cease fire was signed and plans made for the demobilization and disarmament of rebel fighters.[1]

The United Nations Children's Fund has described Angola as "the worst place in the world to be a child." Almost 30 percent of children die before they reach the age of six. Nearly half of all Angolan children are underweight, and a third of school-age children have no school to go to. Adults are hardly better off. Two-thirds of Angolans scrape by on less than a dollar a day, and 42 percent of adults are illiterate. Unsafe drinking water (68 percent of the population lacks access) and a pervasive lack of health services (80 percent have no access to basic medical care) have combined with food shortages to limit life expectancy to 47 years. The 2002 Human Development Index of the UN Development Programme (UNDP), a broad gauge of social and economic progress, ranked Angola 161st out of 173 nations.[2]

Endowed with ample diamond and oil deposits, Angola should not be on the bottom rungs of the world's social ladder. But instead of a blessing, Angola's natural resource wealth has turned out to be a curse. While the majority of the population lived in misery and terror, the leaders of both the government and the rebel UNITA forces devoted most of the money they gained selling Angola's resources to buying weapons and lining their own pockets. The conflict ravaged the economy, displaced close to 4 million people—one out of three Angolans—and left about a million people dependent on foreign food aid. The ideological differences that first sparked the war came to reside in the dustbin of history, but resource-driven greed and corruption proved to be powerful fuel for its continuation.[3]

Though a somewhat extreme case, Angola is merely one of numerous places in the developing world where abundant natural resources help fuel conflicts. (See Appendix 1, page 65.)[4] Altogether, about a quarter of the roughly 50 wars and armed conflicts active in 2001 have a strong resource dimension—in the sense that legal or illegal resource exploitation helped trigger or exacerbate violent conflict or financed its continuation. The human toll of these resource-related conflicts is simply horrendous. Rough estimates suggest that more than 5 million people were killed during the 1990s. Close to 6 million fled to neighboring countries, and anywhere from 11 to 15 million people were displaced inside the borders of their home countries. But some people—warlords, corrupt governments, and unscrupulous corporate leaders—benefited from the pillage, taking in billions of dollars. (See Table 1.)[5]

Since the late 1990s, awareness has grown rapidly of the close links among illegal resource extraction, arms trafficking, violent conflict, human rights violations, humanitarian disaster, and environmental destruction. Expert panels established by the United Nations have investigated cases in Angola, Sierra Leone, and the Democratic Republic of the Congo. Civil society groups have launched a campaign against "conflict diamonds" from those countries and have shed light on other conflict resources as well. Company and industry practices are coming under greater scrutiny. Media reports have helped carry these concerns from activist and specialist circles to a broader audience. All of this also comes against the back-

TABLE 1

Estimated Revenues From Conflict Resources, Selected Cases

Combatant	Resource	Period	Estimated Revenue
UNITA (Angola)	Diamonds	1992–2001	$4–4.2 billion total
RUF (Sierra Leone)	Diamonds	1990s	$25–125 million/year
Taylor (Liberia)	Timber	Late 1990s	$100–187 million/year
Sudan government	Oil	Since 1999	$400 million/year
Rwanda government	Coltan (from Congo)	1999–2000	$250 million total
Taliban (Afghanistan)	Opium, heroin	Mid-1990s–2001	$30–40 million/year
Northern Alliance (Afghanistan)	Lapis lazuli, emeralds, opium	Mid-1990s–2001	$60 million/year
Khmer Rouge (Cambodia)	Timber	Mid-1990s	$120–240 million/year
Cambodia government	Timber	Mid-1990s	$100–150 million/year
Burma government	Timber	1990s	$112 million/year
FARC (Colombia)	Cocaine	Late 1990s	$140 million/year

Source: See Endnote 5.

ground of an intensifying debate over the unchecked proliferation of small arms, the weapons of choice in resource-based conflicts.

In some places, the pillaging of oil, minerals, metals, gemstones, or timber allows wars to continue that were triggered by other factors—initially driven by grievances or ideological struggles and bankrolled by the superpowers or other external supporters. Elsewhere, nature's bounty attracts groups that may claim they are driven by an unresolved grievance, such as political oppression or the denial of minority rights, but are in effect predators enriching themselves through illegal resource extraction. They initiate violence not necessarily to overthrow a government, but to gain and maintain control over lucrative resources, typically one of the few sources of wealth and power in poorer societies. They are greatly aided by the fact that many countries are weakened by poor or repressive governance, crumbling public services, lack of economic opportunity, and deep social divides.

Another dimension to the relationship between resources and conflict concerns the repercussions from resource extraction itself. In many developing countries, the economic benefits of mining and logging operations accrue to a small business or government elite and to foreign investors. But in case after case, an array of burdens—ranging from the expropriation of land, disruption of traditional ways of life, environmental devastation, and social maladies—are shouldered by the local population. Typically, these communities are neither informed nor consulted about resource extraction projects. This has led to violent conflict in places like Nigeria's Niger Delta, Bougainville in Papua New Guinea, and several provinces in Indonesia. Rather than full-fledged war, these conflicts usually involve smaller-scale skirmishes, roadblocks, acts of sabotage, and major human rights violations by state security forces and rebel groups. A number of these conflicts, however, have evolved into secessionist struggles.

These and other cases discussed here are all "civil" conflicts in the sense that the violence takes place within a given country. But there are important global and regional connections—through the world market for illegal resources and the supply of arms, and through spillovers into neighboring countries. And additional global dimensions, in the form of cross-border resource wars, are possible. Although world commodity prices have been weak since the 1970s, a recent study by Professor Michael Klare of Hampshire College argues that as demand for fuels, minerals, water, and other primary commodities continues to rise rapidly, disputes over ownership are multiplying, and the likelihood that industrial powers will intervene to secure "their" supplies of raw materials is increasing.[6]

The types of conflict discussed in this paper are part of a larger set of issues that are marked by a strong resource and environmental dimension. In contrast to the struggles arising out of a context of contested resource *wealth*, there are also a host of other conflicts that emerge from situations of resource *scarcity*—overuse and depletion—and are exacerbated by the social and economic repercussions of environmental degradation. Research during the 1990s has contributed a growing number of case studies of local and regional disputes that revolve around the degradation of arable land, depletion of water for irrigation and human consumption, decimation of forests, and access to other scarce resources.[7]

Some analysts have argued that it is either resource wealth or resource scarcity, but not both, that gives rise to conflict. But this is a false dichotomy, hewing more to the purity of academic theory than allowing for the complexities and contradictions of our world, in which some regions enjoy a generous resource endowment, even as others have to contend with meager resources or have already depleted a large portion of their resource base. Where resource wealth is a factor in conflicts, it is primarily non-renewable resources such as fuels and minerals that are at issue (though a nominally renewable one, such as timber, is important as well). On the other hand, where resource scarcity is a factor, it concerns principally resources that cannot be looted and traded, such as farmland and water. In addition, conditions of resource wealth may co-exist with conditions of depletion and deprivation. The island of Bougainville in the Pacific Ocean, for instance, is extraordinarily rich in copper. Scarcity factors (the environmental devastation from mining operations in the form of contaminated rivers and decimated crop harvests) triggered conflict on the island as much as the wealth factor (disputes over the unjust distribution of the revenues from copper mining).[8]

This paper focuses on resource wealth as a conflict factor. Although such conflicts are fought out in locales far from the Western industrial countries that are the prime consumers of such resources, they relate to a number of key global concerns. As this paper will explain, they affect the wellbeing and future prospects of many millions of people; play an important role in the damage visited upon several biodiversity hotspots; challenge fledgling efforts to control the proliferation of arms and to advance conflict resolution and peacekeeping; demonstrate the importance (and fragile status) of human rights; highlight the importance of good governance and economic diversification; and raise troubling questions about corporate accountability and the role of the globalizing economy.

The Nature of Resource Conflicts

In contrast to the cold war era, today's conflicts are less about ideologies and seizing the reins of state than about the struggle to control or plunder resources—capturing sites rich in minerals, timber, and other valuable commodities or controlling points through which they pass on the way to markets. Paul Collier, director of the Development Research Group at the World Bank, has been one of the earliest to argue that greed and the availability of "lootable" natural resource wealth are key factors.[9]

Although some of today's conflicts have their roots in long-standing grievances, there is a self-sustaining vicious cycle at work in which the spoils of resource exploitation fund war, and war provides the means and conditions that allow continued illegitimate access to these resources. The conflict in the Sudan provides a telling example: Oil exports have permitted the central government to carry on with the war against southern rebels. To keep paying for the war, the government must expand oil production, but this requires exploiting oil deposits deeper and deeper in rebel-held territory. To control oil-rich areas in southern Sudan, government forces are conducting a scorched earth campaign at terrible human cost. Oil finances the war; the war provides access to oil.[10]

When the cold war rivalry came to an end in the late 1980s, much of the support previously extended by the two superpowers to governments and rebel groups among their Third World allies disappeared. External patrons (either governments or nationals living outside the country) have not vanished altogether, but warring factions are increasingly relying on a variety of criminal means, including extortion, pillage, hostage-taking, monopolistic control of trade, drug trafficking, exploitation of coerced labor, and commandeering of humanitarian aid within their borders. But possibly the most important revenue source is the often-illicit extraction and trading of natural resources.[11]

It is difficult to ascertain the share of resources derived

from war zones. For diamonds, industry giant De Beers estimated that in 1999 conflict diamonds accounted for about 4
percent of the world's rough diamond production of $6.8 bil-
lion. But the proportion may have been higher in earlier years,
and some estimates go as high as 20 percent. Conflict diamonds
are part of a broader problem of illicit diamonds—gems that
have been mined illegally or stolen, but not derived from
conflict areas. A UN group of experts estimated in 2000 that
about 20 percent of the global trade in rough diamonds is
illicit.[12]

It is extremely difficult to distinguish between conflict,
illicit, and legal gems. Diamonds are easy to conceal and
smuggle across borders. Even in legal transactions, diamonds
of different origin are frequently mixed and remixed as they
are sold and resold, and shipped from one country to another
before reaching their final destination. The industry's lack of
transparency and aversion to outside scrutiny, incomplete
and contradictory trade statistics, and inadequate national
customs regulations add to the difficulty of establishing the true
origin of gemstones.[13]

Concerning timber, Friends of the Earth UK estimated that
as much as 50 percent of tropical timber imports into the
European Union may be illegal; this may be true for a comparable, if not larger, portion of imports worldwide. This is a
product not only of the illicit logging practices in exporting
countries, but also the fact that importing industrial countries
have no laws on the books that would outlaw the import of
such commodities. [14]

LOOTABILITY AND OBSTRUCTABILITY: FACTORS IN RESOURCE EXPLOITATION

Both state- and non-state groups have commonly used natural resources to finance military activities. Non-state groups
include secessionist movements and rebels fighting to overthrow a government as well as regional warlords and predatory
groups that are more criminal than political in their motives.
Non-state groups have sought to pillage existing stocks of

minerals, gems, or agricultural raw materials. They have awarded illegal concessions to companies willing to contract with them. They press large numbers of civilians into mining and logging operations or put some of their own combatants to work. Sometimes, they are content to "tax" those engaged in resource extraction, or to extract ransom before allowing the passage of commodities to their intended markets.

Although governments' reliance on natural resource deposits to fund military operations would seem to be a simple exercise of sovereign right, there are often questionable or even illegal aspects to such actions. In the first place, the democratic legitimacy of some regimes is in question. More specifically, concessions are sometimes awarded in ways that bend or circumvent applicable laws. Revenue streams are kept off the books and end up not only purchasing arms and military equipment but also enriching corrupt elites, as happened in Angola, Liberia, and Cambodia. In some cases, such as in the Sudan, government troops are using extreme violence to de-populate resource-rich areas and keep them securely in government hands.

A number of factors influence whether a government or a non-state group is able to capture and exploit a given resource. Philippe Le Billon of the International Institute for Security Studies in London makes a distinction between proximate and distant resources. The more distant a resource is from the center of government control, the more difficult it is for the government to maintain control over the resource vis-à-vis an opposition force. A second distinction concerns point resources and diffuse resources. An example can be found in the diamond industry. Kimberlite diamonds are found in fairly concentrated locations, whereas alluvial diamonds can be found in riverbeds stretching over wide territories. A point resource is more easily controlled by one side to a conflict, whereas a diffuse resource may benefit a range of contenders.[15]

Further, there are questions of "lootability" and "obstructability." Governments tend to have the capacity to extract whatever resource is found on their territory (if need be, relying on the technical expertise and capital of private companies). By contrast, rebel or warlord forces often have limited technical and financial capabilities. But some types of resources lend themselves more easily to plunder than others. Logging, for example, is a relatively straightforward activity, offering a quick return for very little investment. A small number of combatants equipped with chainsaws and trucks can generate a substantial flow of revenues. Large-scale mining operations are beyond the abilities of non-government forces and are hence less lootable, but alluvial diamond deposits are accessible even to those without sophisticated technologies and heavy-duty equipment. Oil, particularly from offshore fields, is virtually impervious to rebel pillage.[16]

Obstructability—the ability to block the shipment of a natural resource to processing plants or markets—is an additional important factor. As Le Billon points out, "unlike manufacturing and to some extent agriculture, primary resource exploitation activities cannot be relocated. Although resource businesses may decide not to invest or to disengage from their current operations, they generally sustain their access to resources and protect their investments by paying whoever is in power— ranging from a few dollars to let a truck pass a check-point, to multi-million-dollar concession signature bonuses paid to belligerents." In Colombia and Sudan, rebels have used actual or threatened oil pipeline bombings to extort payments from the government and oil companies.[17]

Professor Michael Ross of the University of California at Los Angeles has examined whether resource wealth has had an impact on the incidence, duration, and intensity of several recent or ongoing conflicts. He finds that resource wealth plays an important role in the outbreak of conflict and tends to make conflicts last longer, but has a more mixed influence on their intensity. In one case, the long-running civil war in Sudan, resource wealth has played an unambiguous role in all three aspects.[18] (See Table 2, page 15.)

Most of the violence in resource-related conflicts is directed against civilians. Since establishing undisputed control over resources is a key objective, armed groups seek to intimidate the local population into submission or use terror to drive people away. "Hence the importance of extreme and conspicuous atrocity," observes Mary Kaldor of the University of Sussex, including directly expelling people, rendering an area uninhabitable by the indiscriminate spread of landmines, shelling houses and hospitals, chopping off people's limbs, imposing long sieges and blockades to induce famine, and inflicting systematic sexual violence. Unlike ideologically based movements, those pursuing resource wealth do not compete for the hearts and minds of the local population. Young boys are often turned into child soldiers, and girls into sex slaves for older fighters. Many combatants are forced to commit atrocities, often against their own relatives, in order to traumatize them and to spread a sense of complicity that will prevent them from being accepted back into their communities later.[19]

Actions that are often described as chaos, collapse, and senseless violence in media reports actually flow from a certain logic, albeit a perverted one. David Keen, a lecturer at the London School of Economics, argues that violence serves an economic function, maintaining a conflict economy that benefits certain groups—government officials, warlords, combatants, arms smugglers, and unscrupulous traders and business people. Those who benefit from this violent "mode of accumulation" derive profit, power, and status, even as it spells impoverishment, broken lives, and death for society at large. Groups living off a lucrative resource have a vested interest in maintaining the status quo and, if need be, in prolonging conflict. They are likely to find this to be a more attractive choice than settling conflict because it allows them to maintain their privileged position and bestows a quasi-legitimacy on their actions.[20]

THE RESOURCE CURSE

Why are some countries susceptible to resource-based conflicts? While the availability and lootability of natural resources are key factors, they alone do not explain the matter. Many countries with rich resource endowments, such as Australia and

TABLE 2

The Impact of Resource Wealth on Armed Conflict, 16 Cases

Conflict Location	Period	Key Characteristics of Conflict	Impact of Resource Wealth on:		
			Conflict Initiation	Conflict Duration	Conflict Intensity
Afghanistan	1979–2001	Resource looting	No	Prolonged	No
Angola	1975–2002	Looting, resource battles, coop. plunder	No	Prolonged	Mixed
Angola (Cabinda)	1975–present	Grievances	Yes	None	No
Burma	1949–present	Resource looting, incentive, resource battles, coop. plunder	No	Unclear	Mixed
Cambodia	1978–97	Looting, resource battles, coop. plunder, lack of cohesion	No	Unclear	Mixed
Colombia	1984–present	Looting, resource battles, coop. plunder	No	Prolonged	Mixed
Republic of Congo	1997	Looting, incentive	Yes	Shortened	No
Zaïre	1996–97	Predatory groups, looting	Yes	Shortened	No
Democratic Republic of the Congo	1998–present	Looting, resource battles, coop. plunder, disincentive	Yes	Prolonged	Mixed
Indonesia (Aceh)	1975–present	Grievances, repression	Yes	None	Yes
Indonesia (West Papua)	1969–present	Repression	No	None	Yes
Liberia	1989–96	Looting, resource battles, coop. plunder, lack of cohesion, disincentive	No	Prolonged	Mixed
Papua New Guinea (Bougainville)	1988–98[1]	Grievances	Yes	None	No
Peru	1980–95	Resource looting, resource battles	No	Prolonged	Yes
Sierra Leone	1991–2000	Looting, predatory groups, resource battles, coop. plunder	Yes	Prolonged	Mixed
Sudan	1983–present	Looting, grievances, resource battles, coop. plunder, repression	Yes	Prolonged	Yes
No. of conflicts where resource wealth has had an impact:			8	8 prolonged 2 shortened	4 (plus 7 mixed)

[1] Cease-fire, followed by peace agreement in 2001.
See Endnote 18 for source and an explanation of terms.

Botswana, have not fallen prey to violence. Where conflict does break out, it is the result of a combination of factors—political, social, economic, and military—that make for weak, though typically repressive and undemocratic, states and vulnerable economies.

Ample resource endowments can have negative economic consequences, as countries grow overly dependent on these resources, allocate inadequate capital and labor to other sectors—agriculture, manufacturing, and services—and underinvest in critical social areas such as education and health. The result is a failure to diversify the economy and to stimulate innovation and the development of human skills.

Examining the world's most oil- and minerals-dependent states, Jeffrey Sachs and Andrew Warner found that they tend to experience lower economic growth than countries less reliant on such commodities. More important, the type of growth is often ill-suited to the needs of the majority of the population: being capital-intensive, extractive industries provide only a limited number of jobs, and many of those go to skilled technicians from developed countries.[21]

Resource extraction industries tend to have "enclave" characteristics, i.e., they create only small pockets of wealth and have few linkages to the rest of the national economy, particularly if the resources are exported before any processing takes place. The benefits to the economy and population at large are therefore quite limited. Frequently, enclaves are even physically separated, as mineral deposits or timber resources are often found in remote areas; some oil resources, for instance, are located offshore.[22]

Furthermore, worsened by the volatility of world commodity market prices, extractive industries follow a disruptive boom-and-bust cycle. Projected revenues from commodity exports are often used as collateral for loans, yet projections may prove overly optimistic and world market prices can unexpectedly decline; indeed, non-fuel commodity prices have been on a downward slide since the mid-1970s. (See Figure 1, page 19.) As a result, foreign debt balloons, and if the loans were used for unproductive purposes (as is often the case), repayment becomes problematic. According to Michael Ross, 12 of the world's 25 most mineral-dependent states, and 6 of the world's 25 most oil-dependent states, are among the group of countries categorized by the World Bank as "highly indebted poor countries."[23]

Ross's statistical analysis finds that the more that countries depend on exporting minerals, the worse they score on UNDP's Human Development Index. Specifically, they under-achieve in terms of under-5 mortality rates, life expectancy at birth, and child education. And they also experience significantly higher levels of inequality between rich and poor than other countries with comparable levels of income. Oil-dependent states experience a similar, though somewhat less pronounced, situation.[24]

This outcome is not mere coincidence. Societies whose main income is derived from resource royalties instead of value added seem prone to develop a culture with widespread corruption. Resource royalties enable political leaders to maintain their stranglehold on power by funding a system of patronage that rewards followers and punishes opponents. And because such regimes rely less on revenues derived from a broad-based system of taxation, they also have less need for popular legitimacy and feel less pressure to be accountable. [25]

Professor William Reno of Northwestern University has christened the extremely poor governance of many countries a "shadow state": corruption and patronage are rife, public goods and services are withheld from most people, and state institutions (like the civil service, universities, the central bank) are deliberately weakened to thwart potential challengers to the ruler, while a parallel network outside these formal institutions is created for the benefit of leaders and their cronies. State revenues are diverted to generate huge illicit fortunes for rulers that are used for patronage payments to key regime supporters. The kleptocracy under Zaïre's dictator Mobutu serves as a prime example of this phenomenon.[26]

The allocation of oil, minerals, or forest resource concessions to regime supporters is both a scheme for corruption and private enrichment and a crucial mechanism to turn resources into cashable wealth that helps prop up the existing regime through the purchase of arms and the maintenance of armed forces. Many governments of resource-rich countries spend a very high proportion of state income on internal security to suppress democratic movements or other challenges to their power. Often, revenues from logging or mining operations are kept off the official national budget, and in some cases the operators are providing illicit services to the regime, such as running guns. This was done in Liberia under Charles Taylor, for instance.[27]

THE PROLIFERATION OF ARMS AND COMBATANTS

Rulers of shadow states often foster and manipulate conflicts among different communities, factions, and ethnic groups as a means to maintain control. However, ruling in such a fashion intensifies frictions within society. In such conditions, discontented and aggrieved groups turn increasingly to protest and perhaps violence, rivals rise to challenge the discredited leadership, and ruthless political-criminal entrepreneurs who sense an opportunity for pillaging resources use violence to achieve their objective. In a country with a poorly developed and diversified economy, with few resources other than rich veins of minerals or vast tracts of forest, and without democratic means of governing, seizing control of a prized resource is the ticket to wealth and power.[28]

In many developing countries, particularly in sub-Saharan Africa, government forces are in decay and private security organizations are on the rise, including forces loyal to regional warlords, citizens' self-defense groups, corporate-sponsored forces, foreign mercenaries, and criminal gangs. In fact, it is becoming more difficult to make clear-cut distinctions between legitimate and illegitimate, and between public and private, security forces.

This is happening for a number of reasons. Without cold war-motivated sponsorship and under increasing pressure from western donors to tighten belts, many governments can

FIGURE 1

Composite Non-Fuel Commodity Prices, 1960–2001

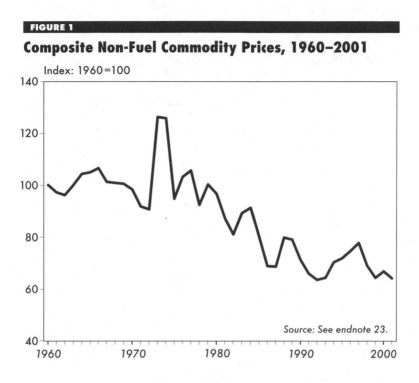

Index: 1960=100

Source: See endnote 23.

no longer maintain large armies. Soldiers go unpaid or under-paid and often turn to other sources of funding, including plunder and extortion. Such fragmentation is even more likely where rulers have deliberately created rival security forces that keep each other in check, preventing a serious challenge to central control. Some military commanders become de facto local warlords, establishing quasi-commercial logging, mining, or drug-producing fiefdoms.[29]

During the 1990s, a number of private military firms rose to prominence. Companies like Executive Outcomes, Sandline International, Defense Systems Ltd., and Ghurka Security Guards attracted military personnel from western industrial and former Warsaw Pact armies who lost their jobs at the end of the cold war, as well as veterans of apartheid-era South Africa. They offer a range of services, including training, consulting, and guarding of facilities and mercenary activities such as procuring or brokering weapons and running combat operations. Several beleaguered governments, including those of Angola, Sierra Leone, and Papua New Guinea, turned to them to help fight rebel groups, paying them with revenues derived from natural resources or, in some cases, granting them (or affiliated companies) concessions to diamonds and other resources.[30]

Multinational oil and mining corporations often rely on private security forces to guard their operations and facilities. Companies like Occidental Petroleum in Colombia, Shell in Nigeria, Talisman Energy in Sudan, and ExxonMobil and Freeport-McMoRan in Indonesia have subsidized or helped train and arm government security forces or have made equipment and facilities available. These units have been involved in severe human rights violations.[31]

The massive proliferation of small arms and light weapons plays a key role in all of this. Resource-based conflicts are primarily carried out with such weapons because they are cheap, widely available, easy to conceal and smuggle, and easy to use and maintain. There is considerable uncertainty about the numbers, but an estimated 8 million pistols, revolvers, rifles, submachine guns, and machine guns were manufactured in 2000 (of these, just under 1 million were military-style weapons, the rest were commercial firearms). Estimates are evolving, but it is thought that at least 638 million small arms and light weapons exist worldwide. At least 15 billion rounds of ammunition were produced in 2000 alone. The picture that emerges is one of a world exceedingly well equipped with these tools of terror and death.[32]

Because many activities along the resource-conflict spectrum are illicit and involve actors of questionable legitimacy, grey- and black-market transfers carry special significance. The trafficking of arms is closely linked to illegal trade in raw materials such as minerals, timber, and diamonds. Arms and commodities often travel on the same routes, in opposite directions. Revenues from commodity sales finance the purchase of arms, ammunition, military equipment, uniforms, and other items; sometimes weapons are directly bartered for natural resources, drugs, animal products, and other commodities.[33]

Resource-based conflicts in remote parts of the developing world seem far removed from the shopping malls of the western world. But the resources over which so much blood is being shed have consumers in the richest countries as their final destination, no matter how complex and circuitous the networks of delivery are. For consumers, this is easiest to grasp in the case of diamonds, a highly visible and prominently marketed product. For materials like petroleum, timber, copper, and coltan (a valuable ore used in manufacturing myriad electronic devices), the connection is harder to make because they undergo extensive processing before they find their way into complex consumer products. But a portion of the western world's cell phones, furniture and wood products, and jewelry bears the invisible imprint of violence.[34]

It is this strong demand for commodities and the consumer products made from them that makes illegal resource exploitation so lucrative. The enormous expansion of global trade and the growth of associated trading and financial networks have made access to key markets relatively easy for warring groups. They have had little difficulty in establishing international smuggling networks, given either a lack of awareness and scrutiny or a degree of complicity among international traders, manufacturers, and financiers, as well as lax controls in consuming nations.[35]

As the cases discussed in this paper suggest, a large number of corporations—many relatively small and obscure but a few of them well-known, major international companies—have helped perpetuate resource-based conflict, in several ways:
- by purchasing "hot" commodities from combatants
- by operating timber or mining concessions offered by warlords or rebel forces
- by facilitating the shipment of illicit raw materials
- by operating in countries with repressive governments
- by helping to procure arms for government troops that engage in human rights violations

As objectionable as some of these practices may be, they do not necessarily constitute wrongdoing in a legal sense, particularly where companies contract with a recognized government. But at the very least they play an enabling role in situations where the majority of the population suffers from violence and deprivation.

How Conflicts Are Financed by Natural Resource Pillage

The pillaging of commodities—minerals, gems, timber, and others—has made possible the continuation of several violent conflicts in developing countries. Diamonds have been of particular concern in three conflicts discussed in some detail here: Sierra Leone, the Democratic Republic of the Congo, and Angola. It is a bitter irony that these glittering stones, which advertisers work hard to associate with the idea of love and personal commitment, are also connected with gruesome violence.

SIERRA LEONE AND LIBERIA: TRAPPED IN A VICIOUS CYCLE?

Diamonds played a central role in the conflict that devastated Sierra Leone during the 1990s. Ibrahim Kamara, Sierra Leone's UN ambassador, said in July 2000, "We have always maintained that the conflict is not about ideology, tribal, or regional difference.... The root of the conflict is and remains diamonds, diamonds, and diamonds."[36]

Even prior to the 1990s, corruption, cronyism, and illegal mining had squandered the country's diamond riches, to the point where few government services were functioning and educational and economic opportunities were scarce. Sierra Leone became a "model" shadow state. Pressure from international lenders for financial austerity and cuts in the government workforce only worsened the situation. The International Rescue Committee has reported that one-third of all babies in the diamond-rich Kenema District die before age one. UNDP ranked Sierra Leone last on its Human Development Index in 2001.[37]

Throughout the 1990s, Sierra Leone suffered from rebellion, banditry, coups and coup attempts, and seesawing battle fortunes. In March 1991, the Revolutionary United Front (RUF) invaded Sierra Leone from Liberia and seized control of the Kono diamond fields. The RUF had strong backing from Liberian warlord (now president) Charles Taylor. The ranks of the RUF contained disaffected young men from slum areas, illicit diamond miners, Liberian and Burkinabe mercenaries, and others who welcomed the opportunity for pillage and violence. But many others (including a large number of children) were forcibly recruited. Though the RUF professed to act on unresolved grievances, its principal aim was to gain control over the country's mineral wealth. Characterized by banditry and brutality, the rebellion claimed more than 75,000 lives, turned a half-million Sierra Leoneans into refugees, and displaced half of the country's 4.5 million people.[38]

Faced with the RUF rebellion, the government expanded its armed forces from 3,000 to 14,000. This undisciplined, ineffective, ragtag army brought together ill-trained soldiers, militiamen from neighboring Liberia, urban toughs, and street children involved in petty theft. Mary Kaldor of the University of Sussex comments about the latter that "they were given an AK47 and a chance to engage in theft on a larger scale." Government soldiers often supplemented their meager pay through looting and illegal mining.[39]

Rebel forces and parts of the government army actually collaborated at times. Government soldiers by day sometimes became rebels by night. This cooperation between supposed adversaries culminated in May 1997 when disgruntled government soldiers staged a coup against a government that had been elected just a few months earlier, and invited the RUF to join the new junta.[40]

Sierra Leone is a comparatively small diamond producer, but a large share of its gemstones are of very high quality and therefore sought after. The RUF purchased arms and sustained itself through its control of the diamond fields, but diamond wealth has also been a constant source of internal friction. At first, RUF fighters did the mining, but later the group relied more on forced labor, including that of children. The group's annual income has been estimated at $25- to $125 million. RUF diamonds have entered the world market disguised as Liberian, Guinean, and Gambian gemstones.[41]

A UN investigative panel reported conclusive evidence in December 2000 that Burkina Faso is a key conduit in facilitating small arms shipments to Liberia and the RUF. In addition, arms have been transferred through Senegal, Gambia, and Guinea. And Côte d'Ivoire has directly assisted the RUF. Weapons originated primarily in Libya, Ukraine, Slovakia, and Bulgaria, and sometimes were shipped with the help of western air cargo companies. (See Figure 2.)[42]

Charles Taylor's Liberia has played a pivotal role. The UN panel reported that it had found "unequivocal and overwhelming evidence that Liberia has been actively supporting the RUF at all levels, in providing training, weapons and related matériel, logistical support, a staging ground for attacks and a safe haven for retreat and recuperation, and for public relations activities." Under Taylor, Liberia became a major center for diamond smuggling, arms and drug trafficking, and money laundering. The country exported diamonds to Belgium far in excess of the quantity and quality available in Liberia, with gems originating from illicit sources in Sierra Leone and elsewhere.[43]

To the degree that international sanctions succeeded in clamping down on the trade in conflict diamonds, the importance of timber rose in Taylor's calculus. The warlord-turned-president managed to claim Liberia's natural resources as his private domain. Close Taylor associates received the largest concessions in Liberia's forest-rich southeast, where 10 companies control more than 85 percent of the country's total timber production. Liberian timber has been sold primarily in China, but also in France and Italy and to a lesser extent in Spain and the Netherlands. Global Witness estimated that the timber trade was worth at least $100 million in 2000. Only $7 million went to government coffers, even as civil servants went unpaid and the only university remained closed for lack of funds. Most of the money instead went directly to Taylor, into patronage payments, to Taylor-connected paramilitary units that terror-

FIGURE 2

Arms Supply Routes to RUF Rebels in Sierra Leone, 1990s

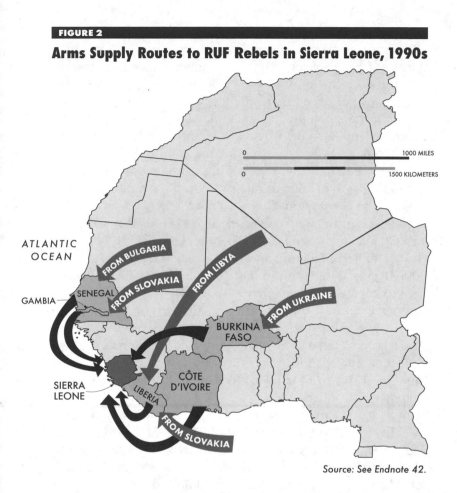

Source: See Endnote 42.

ize the population, and to pay for arms purchases.[44]

At least seven of the logging concessionaires have been involved in procuring arms for the RUF and importing weapons into Liberia in defiance of a UN embargo. One of the concessionaires is Exotic Tropical Timber Enterprise, run by Ukrainian arms and diamond dealer Leonid Minin, who was arrested in Italy in July 2001 for gun-running. But the key player appears to be the Oriental Timber Company (OTC). Controlling 40 to 50 percent of Liberia's forests and its timber production, the company has been implicated in smuggling weapons to the RUF along its timber roads. OTC has not only engaged in rapacious clear-cutting methods, it has also bulldozed homes and entire villages with little warning and no compensation. Meanwhile, social and economic benefits from logging for local communities are close to non-existent. Unemployment is rampant, poverty widespread, and general living conditions desperate. The city of Buchanan, a provincial capital and OTC's base, has no electricity and its sole hospital lacks running water.[45]

Liberia and Charles Taylor are now coming full circle. Having caused havoc in Sierra Leone, his regime is now falling victim to similar dynamics. In April 1999, anti-government rebels crossed into Liberia from Guinea. The insurgency grew, recruiting fighters from Liberia, Guinea, Sierra Leone, Côte d'Ivoire, and Ghana, and combined with other groups into Liberians United for Reconciliation and Democracy (LURD) in February 2000. Fighting flared up in late 2001, and as in Sierra Leone, the victims are mainly civilians. To weaken the Taylor regime, the rebels are not only destroying timber company equipment, but also attacking or occupying many diamond mining districts, and appear to have smuggled diamonds out via Guinea, Gambia, and Sierra Leone. The loss of revenue is making it more difficult for Taylor to pay his military and there is evidence that Liberian army units have been encouraged to plunder certain areas to supplement government payments.[46]

In June 2002, a report by UN Secretary-General Kofi Annan warned of the risk that Liberia and Sierra Leone could be trapped in a vicious cycle, with civil war swinging back and forth between the two countries. With fighting in Liberia escalating, refugee movements and incursions by armed groups from Liberia into Sierra Leone could destabilize the latter country just as it struggles to emerge from a decade of devastation.[47]

DEMOCRATIC REPUBLIC OF THE CONGO: THE NEW WEALTH GRAB

Resource pillage has also been a key factor in the two conflicts that have engulfed the former Zaïre, now called the Democratic Republic of the Congo, in devastating violence since 1996. In the 1996–97 conflict in Zaïre, which ended with the overthrow of the Mobutu dictatorship, the winning side benefited from the politics of resource exploitation. As Laurent Kabila's rebel Alliance of Democratic Forces for the Liberation of Congo-Zaïre (ADFL) gathered strength, international investors negotiated lucrative resource deals with the ADFL, "effectively crowning Laurent Kabila as the de facto leader of then Zaïre while he was still a rebel leader in control of only a small portion of the country," in the words of Dena Montague, a researcher at the Arms Trade Resource Project in New York. Among the investing companies were such major corporations as De Beers, Anglo-American Corporation, Barrick Gold Corporation, Banro American Resources, American Mineral Fields, and Bechtel Corporation. So aggressive was the swarm of mining corporations into rebel-held territories that in some ways it seemed like a replay of the wealth grab in the late 19th century when the Congo came under the control of Belgian colonialism. In April 1997, when it was clear that Kabila's forces had the upper hand, the ADFL signed an $885 million contract with American Mineral Fields, a U.S. firm craving the copper, cobalt, and zinc deposits that had fallen under rebel control. Bechtel provided Kabila with extensive sets of satellite images and infra-red maps of the country's mineral potential free of charge.[48]

The second war has seen far more widespread resource looting, death, and suffering. To date it has killed an estimated 2- to 3 million people and displaced at least another 2 million. In August 1998, Ugandan and Rwandan troops invaded, assisting rebel groups seeking to overthrow the Kabila government. Angola, Zimbabwe, Namibia, and Chad dispatched troops in support of Kabila. According to one estimate, more than 100,000 foreign troops were at one point involved in Congo, though several foreign forces have recently been withdrawn or reduced in size. Political and military factors played an important role in triggering the conflict. Kabila's erstwhile backers, Uganda and Rwanda, quickly grew disenchanted with him. And several of the intervening forces also wanted to thwart their own rebel groups operating from Congolese soil. Rwanda, in particular, was concerned that remnants of the Hutu

Interahamwe militias that had carried out a campaign of genocide in 1994 were using Congo as a staging ground for ongoing hit-and-run attacks.[49]

But whereas the initial motivation was primarily related
to security concerns, the opportunity to plunder the enormous
resource wealth of Congo, in the context of lawlessness and
a weak central authority, soon came to be the primary incentive. Congo is extremely rich in minerals and gemstones such
as diamonds, gold, coltan, niobium, cassiterite, copper, cobalt,
zinc, and manganese. It also offers copious agricultural and
forestry resources such as timber, coffee, tea, and palm oil. In
addition, the country's wildlife, including okapis, gorillas,
and elephants, has long attracted poachers. (See Figure 3.)[50]

During the first year of their invasion, the foreign forces
and their rebel allies resorted to outright plunder of stockpiled
raw materials. Once the stockpiles were exhausted, they organized a variety of methods to extract additional resources. In
some cases, the armies have directly been engaged in resource
extraction; for instance, the Ugandan army has carried out gold
mining activities. Individual soldiers work for their own or their
commanders' benefit, while local Congolese have been put to
work by Rwandan and Ugandan forces. Local artisanal miners
were made to relinquish some of their finds, or were taxed.
Child labor has been used in gold and diamond mining. Occupying forces and their rebel allies have also forced coffee grow-
ers and palm oil producers to sell their commodities at
depressed prices. Last, but not least, companies of questionable
reputation were given concessions to exploit Congo's resources.
An investigation by the Antwerp-based International Peace
Information Service found that a number of Belgian, Dutch,
German, and Swiss companies have been involved in the illegal coltan trade.[51]

The conflict has enabled Rwanda and Uganda to become
major exporters of raw materials that they do not possess at
all or have only in limited quantities. Looted resources have
become a major source of their foreign exchange. Uganda, for
instance, is re-exporting gold, diamonds, cassiterite, coltan, coffee, tea, timber, elephant tusks, and medicinal barks. In 2001

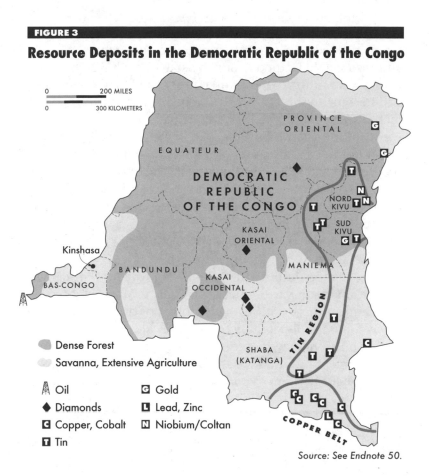

FIGURE 3

Resource Deposits in the Democratic Republic of the Congo

Legend:

- Dense Forest
- Savanna, Extensive Agriculture
- Oil
- Diamonds
- Copper, Cobalt
- Tin
- Gold
- Lead, Zinc
- Niobium/Coltan

Source: See Endnote 50.

it exported 10 times more gold ore than it did five years earlier. Resource pillage has allowed both countries to finance their military presence. Rwanda has even set up an extra-budgetary system for this purpose, and Rwandan President Paul Kagame has described the war as "self-financing." In Uganda's case, the individual enrichment of top military commanders and businessmen—including Salim Saleh, who is the brother of President Museveni, and James Kazini, the former chief of staff of the Ugandan army—appears to be the main driving force.[52]

Kinshasa (the capital) and the Kabila government nearly fell to Rwandan troops at the beginning of the invasion. To stave off defeat and continue the war, the cash-strapped government relied on the country's resources to purchase weapons and secure allied support. But the state-owned mining companies, Gécamines (copper and cobalt) and Miba (diamonds), had become dysfunctional through corruption, mismanagement, theft of equipment and spare parts, and lack of investment during the Mobutu years. Copper production was at one-fifteenth its peak, cobalt output at one-sixth, and diamond production had fallen by almost half. The only way to obtain revenues quickly was to grant concessions ("indiscriminately," in the judgment of a UN panel of experts), and enter into joint ventures with foreign firms in return for up-front payments. Diamonds mined near the city of Mbuji-Mayi, for instance, now bring in about $25 million per month.[53]

Even more importantly, Kabila appealed to Zimbabwe, Angola, and Namibia for military assistance. Although the governments of these nations had strong political and strategic motivations for dispatching troops, they also demanded compensation (Zimbabwe's economy was drained by the military intervention), and Kinshasa used resource wealth as an incentive for its allies to stay involved. The government has granted several concessions, including offshore oil wells to Angola, a share of a diamond mine in Kasai-Occidental province to Namibia, and mining, forestry, and agricultural rights to Zimbabwe.[54]

Angola's and Namibia's commercial pursuits are modest; those of Zimbabwe are far more extensive. The leadership of the Zimbabwean military formed Osleg (Operation Sovereign Legitimacy), a company that was supposed to pay for the military presence in Congo. Osleg secured timber rights to as much as 33 million hectares of land, or about 15 percent of Congo's total territory. Osleg also became involved in running the Sengamines diamond concession (including alluvial deposits near Mbuji-Mayi and kimberlite deposits in Tshibua), refurbishing a manganese-oxide processing plant, and operating several timber sawmills. Ridgepoint Overseas Developments, a Zimbabwean firm whose officials include Zimbabwe's justice minister and a nephew of President Mugabe, was awarded management of three Gécamines copper- and cobalt mines.[55]

Zimbabwe's contribution to a variety of resource ventures was primarily in providing troops to keep resource-rich Kasai and Katanga provinces under control. It needed to bring in outside investors for capital and expertise. Among them are companies from Kenya and Tanzania, and large mining conglomerates from South Africa, including Anglo-American. The Sengamines concession, for instance, attracted investment by Oryx Natural Resources, a British-Omani company that in turn is owned by a South African diamond firm.[56]

Responsibility for the conflict in the Congo lies with not only regional leaders but also more distant countries, international donors, and private companies that have wittingly or unwittingly facilitated the exploitation of Congolese resources by shipping and buying illegally obtained commodities. Kenya, Tanzania, Zambia, South Africa, the Central African Republic, and the Republic of Congo are important transit countries, through which illicit Congolese resources reach their markets in industrial countries. A UN expert panel listed 34 companies based in Western Europe, Canada, Malaysia, India, Pakistan, and Russia as importers of such commodities.[57]

The different armed groups in the Congo have long used the presence of their respective opponents as an excuse to justify their own continued occupation of parts of the country. However, a substantial portion of the foreign troops has been withdrawn (Angola, Namibia, Chad, and Burundi have pulled out; Zimbabwe has said it will do the same, but is reluctant; Rwanda and Uganda signed accords with the Congo government to withdraw their soldiers, although it remains to be seen whether they carry out their pledge.) The withdrawals are the result of growing international pressure and the rising cost of the military interventions. While this is good news, it does not necessarily mean that the pillaging of the country's resources is coming to an end. Illegal commercial networks are being left behind as troops withdraw or re-deploy; headed by military officers and unscrupulous political and business leaders, they continue to control vast areas of Congo and operate them as their personal fiefdoms.[58]

ANGOLA: DIAMONDS VERSUS OIL

Angola's involvement in the Congo war is but the most recent episode in its own history of seemingly interminable conflict. Angola has been almost continuously at war since its independence struggle against Portugal (1961–75). At first, it was superpower support (and Cuban and South African intervention) that sustained fighting between the MPLA (Popular Movement for the Liberation of Angola) government and UNITA rebels. But when the outside powers phased out their assistance in the late 1980s, both sides turned to the country's ample natural resources. Three cease-fires and peacemaking efforts failed, primarily because UNITA reneged on its commitments and returned to war. The country now has perhaps the best chance to emerge from its long ordeal. Following Jonas Savimbi's death and a considerable weakening of his forces, the two warring sides signed a cease-fire in April 2001. The rebels agreed to undergo disarmament, demobilization, and reintegration.[59]

Up until then, Angola's oil and diamond wealth fueled arms purchases and enriched a small elite on both sides. Angola is the world's fifth-largest producer of nonindustrial diamonds and the second-largest oil producer in sub-Saharan Africa. Its oil production quadrupled to about 800,000 barrels per day during the 1980s and 1990s. While the offshore oil wells have remained in government hands, control of the diamond mines has shifted back and forth. Both sides have succeeded in mortgaging the country's natural bounty in pursuit of a crippling conflict, severely clouding prospects of future generations.[60]

UNITA derived an estimated $3.7 billion from diamond sales from 1992 through 1998. Early in the decade, UNITA controlled about 90 percent of Angola's diamond exports, but after a string of defeats its share declined to about two-thirds in 1996 and 1997. After 1998, its revenues further declined due to additional territorial losses, depletion of some deposits, and the (limited) impact of UN sanctions. As a result, it is believed that UNITA's diamond income declined to an estimated $80- to $150 million per year, down from as much as $600 million annually a decade ago. Diamond dollars purchased weapons, fuel, and food for troops, but have also been used to curry favor with the leaders of Burkina Faso, Togo, and the former Zaïre. A considerable portion of the income has apparently been siphoned off by corruption.[61]

UNITA had some of its own people involved in diamond digging, but much of the mining has been carried out by an estimated 100,000 bonded laborers, semi-enslaved diggers deprived of even basic rights and working under dangerous conditions. The rebel group also received "commissions" from diamond buyers operating in its realm.[62]

Until 1999, when De Beers decided to stop buying Angolan diamonds, UNITA had little difficulty selling its gemstones. For several years, De Beers pursued a no-questions-asked diamond-purchasing policy, being more interested in maintaining its market control than in the suffering that "blood diamonds" perpetuate. In 1996 and 1997, Angolan diamonds are thought to have accounted for about one-fifth of De Beers' business.[63]

Diverse smuggling routes enabled UNITA to largely circumvent a 1998 UN embargo on its diamonds. Burkina Faso, Zaïre (until the fall of the Mobutu dictatorship), and Rwanda (since 1998) have served as safe havens for illicit transactions. UNITA was able to smuggle diamonds through the Central African Republic, Côte d'Ivoire, Morocco, Namibia, South Africa, and Zambia, with or without the knowledge of the governments of these countries. The Zambian Ministry of Mines, for instance, provided false certificates of origin. The origin of UNITA gemstones was further disguised by having them polished, most likely in Israel and Ukraine.[64]

UNITA was similarly able to evade a UN arms embargo by relying on a variety of arms brokers and delivery routes and by securing the complicity of several governments that provided false end-user certificates for weapons. Mobutu's Zaïre, Burkina Faso, and Togo (from 1996) were major conduits for arms; Zaïre and the Republic of Congo were also used to store UNITA weapons. After 1998, Rwanda allowed UNITA to hold meetings with arms brokers in its capital, Kigali. Weapons—mostly small arms, but also including major items such as tanks and artillery—came primarily from Bulgaria and other East European countries. (See Figure 4).[65]

What diamonds are to UNITA, oil is to the Angolan government. At $2 billion to $3 billion per year, oil revenue accounts for about 90 percent of Angolan exports and a similar share of the government's budget. Oil money has bought arms and kept the war going, particularly in 1993 and 1994, after UNITA captured most of the diamond fields and threatened to vanquish the government army. Almost three times as much budget money has been allocated to the war as to social programs. Meanwhile, a small elite surrounding President Eduardo dos Santos and his top generals has raked in considerable profits through corrupt oil and weapons contracts, control over the allocation of scarce foreign-exchange and import licenses, and other opaque financial deals. For these individuals, the war was lucrative.[66]

Many of the world's largest oil firms, including Chevron, Elf Aquitaine, BP, and ExxonMobil, operate in Angola. Global Witness, a British nongovernmental organization (NGO), charges that the oil companies have been complicit in perpetuating the war because they provided the necessary revenues. Much of the nearly $900 million in signature bonuses that these companies were required to pay in order to secure exploration and production rights in ultra-deep offshore blocks in the late 1990s was apparently used to buy arms. The consortia of companies that were awarded two of these blocks, led by Elf and Exxon, include firms that have been involved in arms dealing.[67]

But in addition to such payments, since the mid-1980s the Angolan government has resorted to securing loans from international banks by mortgaging future oil production. Much of the money from these high-interest loans has financed military spending. A substantial portion of oil revenues flows directly into a foreign bank account for debt servicing instead of being available for badly needed social expenditures. Much of the revenues—more than two-thirds in 1997—is channeled

FIGURE 4

Arms Supply Routes to UNITA Rebels in Angola, 1990s

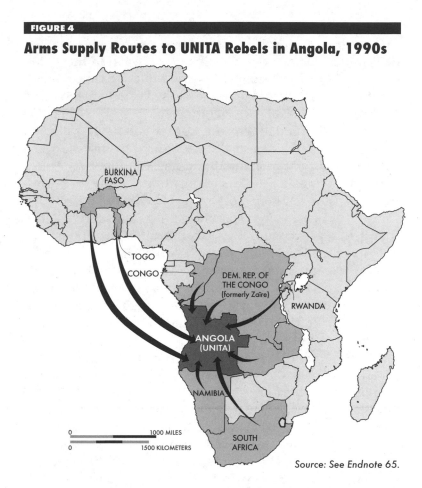

Source: See Endnote 65.

outside the official budget, with little financial accountability and plentiful opportunities for corruption.[68]

COLOMBIA: NARCOTICS, PETROLEUM, AND INDIGENOUS PEOPLES

Unlike Angola, Congo, and Sierra Leone, Colombia has not seen full-scale war, but a long-running lower-intensity type of violence that now threatens to escalate. Newly-elected President Álvaro Uribe plans to double the army's combat force to 100,000 soldiers and is attempting to build a vast force of

civilian informers, possibly armed. Although the civil war in
Colombia has its roots primarily in the struggle for social justice and ideological confrontations that began in the 1940s,
in later years it has been fueled—and prolonged and complicated—to a significant extent by a fight over natural resources:
cocaine and crude oil. (See Figure 5.)[69]

Repression and the growing concentration of wealth and
power in the hands of a small elite spurred the rise of several
leftist guerrilla groups in the 1960s. The Revolutionary Armed
Forces of Colombia (FARC) is mainly based in the coca-grow-
ing regions of southern Colombia. The National Liberation
Army (ELN) operates mostly in the oil-rich northeast. Together,
they field approximately 20,000 combatants. In response, the
military created and supported right-wing paramilitary groups
that became notorious for massacres of civilians. Their 10,000
fighters are believed to be responsible for as many as three-quar-
ters of all political killings. In 1996, these rightist groups
joined with drug lords' private militias to form the United Self
Defense Forces of Colombia (AUC).[70]

Since the 1980s, drug production and trade have
expanded tremendously. Colombia is today the world's largest
supplier of cocaine (90 percent of the crop goes to the United
States), and all factions in the civil war benefit financially. The
FARC "taxes" coca cultivation and production (earning an
estimated $140 million annually), and parts of the FARC and
the ELN are assumed to be involved in drug-trafficking, sup-
plementing their income from kidnappings and extortion.
The AUC paramilitary groups are believed to receive as much
as 70 percent of their funding from drug trafficking.[71]

Increasingly, oil money has also become key to the ongoing civil war. Colombia became a net exporter in 1986, and oil
now accounts for one-third of the country's total export earnings. For the government, it is a critical resource (not least
because Colombia has come under increasing pressure from the
International Monetary Fund to accelerate oil development so
it can pay its foreign debts).[72]

The rebel groups have sought to exact payments from oil
firms and others. The ELN, for instance, levies a 5 percent "tax"

FIGURE 5

Oil Pipelines and Drug Cultivation in Colombia

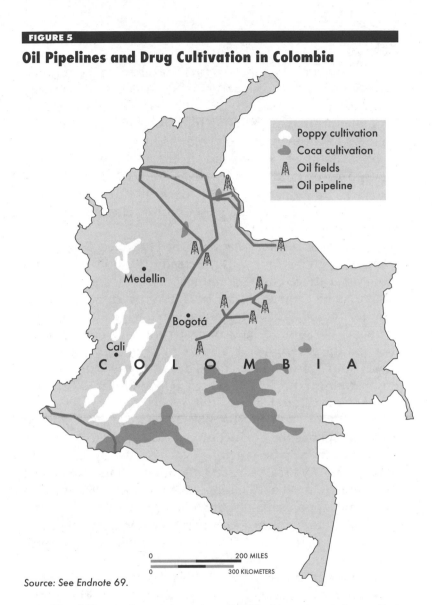

Poppy cultivation
Coca cultivation
Oil fields
— Oil pipeline

Medellin

Bogotá

Cali

C O L O M B I A

0   200 MILES
0   300 KILOMETERS

Source: See Endnote 69.

on all public works projects in oil-rich Arauca province. But the rebels have also sought to cut into the government's oil income by obstructing the flow of oil and deterring additional foreign investment in the oil sector. Since 1986, they have attacked one of the country's key pipelines, Caño Limón,

more than 900 times. Jointly owned by state-owned Ecopetrol
and Los Angeles-based Occidental Petroleum, the pipeline
transports about 35 million barrels of oil annually, running
770 kilometers from the border of Venezuela to Colombia's
Caribbean port of Coveñas. Over the years, the attacks caused
2.6 million barrels of oil to spill into lakes, rivers, and the soil.
The ELN has been careful to avoid totally shutting down the
pipeline. But the FARC has had less reason for restraint, step-
ping up its own attacks in part to deny the rival ELN oil
extortion money. During 2001, attacks put the pipeline out
of operation for a record 266 days, costing close to $600 mil-
lion in foregone revenue.[73]

The government has naturally tried to protect the pipeline
from rebel attack, not only to steady the flow of oil and
money, but also to ensure that foreign oil companies invest in
additional oil exploration. In 1992, the government levied a
"war tax" of more than $1 per barrel on foreign oil companies
to finance the army's defense of the pipeline and other oil facilities. But the government is also counting on far greater assistance from Washington. Lobbied hard by Occidental, the
Bush administration is following a policy similar to that laid
down by the Clinton administration, making available growing amounts of aid to the Colombian military in a two-pronged
effort to suppress the production of coca and protect the flow
of oil—and in the process getting ever more deeply drawn into
the civil war. For fiscal year 2003, the administration requested
$573 million in aid to Colombia. This includes $98 million to
train and support a 2,000- to 4,000-member brigade of the
Colombian army assigned to protect the Caño Limón pipeline.
Restrictions that limited U.S. aid to counter-narcotics programs are more and more being relaxed.[74]

The conflict over oil is affecting Colombia's indigenous
populations, including the U'wa. One of 80 minority ethnic
groups, they have already seen their population dwindle from
20,000 in 1940 to 5,000 today as a result of government
repression and expropriations of about 85 percent of their
ancestral lands. With the support of solidarity groups worldwide, the U'wa have resisted Occidental Petroleum's attempts

to drill for oil on ancestral land adjacent to their current reservation since the early 1990s. According to the Rainforest Action Network, the U'wa homeland in Colombia's Sierra Nevada de Cocuy mountains (northeast of Bogotá) is a delicate cloudforest ecosystem and home to numerous rare and endangered species of plants and animals.[75]

In 1999, the government granted a drilling permit to Occidental without consulting the U'wa, thus violating Colombian law. (A temporary injunction against the drilling plans granted by a lower court was overturned by the Superior Court of Bogotá.) The military forcibly ejected several hundred U'wa who had assembled at the proposed drill site in protest, and occupied the area. Other protests were met with military and police repression. Occidental began drilling operations, protected by thousands of army troops, in November 2000. But the company announced in May 2002 that it would relinquish the drill site, after having failed to find commercially viable oil deposits.[76]

But the U'wa still fear getting caught up in Colombia's oil-related violence. The Caño Limón pipeline runs just north of U'wa territory in northeastern Colombia, and the escalation of violence surrounding the pipeline may entangle the group against its better judgment.[77]

How Resource Extraction Can Trigger Conflict

In many instances, resource extraction is itself the source of conflict. Around the world, the operations of oil, mining, and logging companies are causing severe tensions with local populations, often indigenous communities. In Ecuador and Peru, in Nigeria and Cameroon, and in Indonesia and Papua New Guinea, broadly similar scenarios of environmental destruction, economic inequity, and social alienation are unfolding.

Typically, these operations confiscate land from local people without proper compensation. They cause an array of

environmental problems by poisoning drinking water, destroying arable land, clear-cutting forests, and despoiling hunting
and fishing grounds. And they introduce social disruptions and
communal tensions: roads etched into previously inaccessible
areas bring a heavy influx of construction workers, miners, loggers, and, sometimes, migrant populations. While the burdens
and disruptions are all too real, the economic benefits from
resource extraction mostly accrue to outsiders: the central
government, multinational corporations, and assorted foreign investors. But when the affected communities resist, they
are often met with severe government repression.

INDONESIA: THE SUHARTO LEGACY

Indonesia features some of the most intense resource-trig-
gered struggles, which are to a large extent the product of policies pursued during the long years of the Suharto dictatorship
(1966–98). Under Suharto, licenses were awarded to domestic
and foreign businesses that were closely linked to or broadly
supportive of the regime. In part because this practice was heav-
ily tinged by corruption and favoritism, it brought about pre-
cisely the kind of imbalance of benefits and burdens described
above, and with it, the seeds of conflict. And the Suharto-era
policy of "transmigration"—encouraging the movement of people from the most densely populated parts of the country to
outlying provinces—has added fuel to an already combustible
situation. (See Figure 6.)
        Since 1998, the rapid growth in illegal resource extraction
has complicated the picture and added new strains of conflict.
The Indonesian military and police are involved in both legal
ventures and illegal logging and mining conducted through
front companies and joint ventures with private timber barons.
These activities, along with protection rackets under which illegal operators pay to avoid prosecution, raise half or more of
their operational budgets.[78]
        The province of Aceh, located at the northern tip of
Sumatra, has seen increasing violence. Aceh is home to Arun,
Indonesia's second-largest gas field and the site of a huge liq-

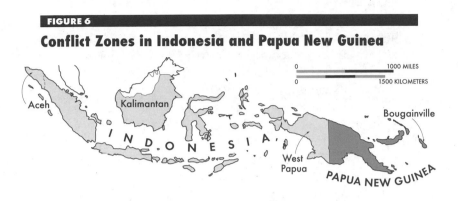

FIGURE 6

Conflict Zones in Indonesia and Papua New Guinea

uefied natural gas plant. Operated by ExxonMobil and owned by the state company Pertamina, Arun generates 30 percent of the country's oil and gas export income, or about $1.2 billion a year. The facility gave rise to local resentments in a number of ways. Construction in the late 1970s displaced several villages and hundreds of families. Gas leaks and chemical spills caused health and environmental problems, devastating local communities depending on agriculture and fish farming.[79]

Aceh is also rich in timber, minerals, and fertile land. These resources, too, were exploited by cronies of the Suharto dictatorship. Land traditionally owned by indigenous people was expropriated; deforestation resulting from excessive logging has caused landslides and flooding and has destroyed homes and rice paddies. Transmigrants from Java that came to Aceh under Suharto to set up timber, pulp, and wood-processing industries have also been a source of intense resentment for the Acehnese.[80]

The Aceh Freedom Movement, known as GAM (Gerakan Aceh Merdeka), began in 1976, but its first uprising was easily crushed by the military. A second rebellion in the late 1980s met with arrests, torture, and rape; it is estimated that more than a thousand civilians were killed by the military. Aceh was put under martial law from 1990 to 1998, but the fall of the Suharto regime allowed exiled GAM guerrillas to return. Some 2,000 fighters face about 21,000 government soldiers and 12,000 police. Renewed violence has killed about 2,000 people, mostly civilians, in 2001, and several thousand more in earlier years. The Indonesian military has pushed the GAM rebels out of urban centers; it routinely carries out arbitrary arrests, torture, disappearances, reprisal killings, and other human rights violations. The Indonesian government is considering declaring a state of emergency that would give the military an even freer hand. Though support for autonomy or independence for Aceh runs high among the province's population of 4.5 million, many are as wary of the GAM as they are of the military, given the abuses committed by both sides.[81]

GAM guerrillas have long targeted military installations and Javanese migrants, but ExxonMobil has also become a prime target. Intensifying attacks forced the company to suspend operations from March to July 2001, costing the government an estimated $100 million in lost revenue per month. Military commanders responded with a counterinsurgency operation that resulted in numerous executions and disappearances and that led thousands of Acehnese to flee their homes. More than 3,000 Indonesian soldiers are now protecting the plant and patrolling its surroundings.[82]

ExxonMobil has sought to portray itself as an innocent bystander of the violence, but NGOs have charged the company with a "complicity of silence" in the face of severe military abuses. Several mass graves have been discovered. Activists allege that ExxonMobil paid the military to provide security for its operations, provided equipment to dig the mass graves, and allowed its facilities to be used by the military for torture and other activities. In July 2001, the Washington-based International Labor Rights Fund filed a lawsuit in the United States against the company on behalf of 11 Acehnese villagers, suing for complicity in murder, torture, kidnapping, and sexual abuse by Indonesian soldiers. At the company's request, however, the Bush administration has asked that the suit be dismissed (as of early September 2002, the judge's decision on whether to proceed was still pending).[83]

Some 5,000 kilometers to the east, in Indonesia's West Papua (formerly known as Irian Jaya), resource wealth helped trigger a conflict that began even earlier. After the area was forcibly incorporated into Indonesia in 1961, a rebel movement known as OPM (Organisasi Papua Merdeka, the Papuan Freedom Organization) arose in the mid-1960s and advocated the establishment of a separate state. But OPM did not gain much support from the local population until the 1970s, when it harnessed grievances against a large-scale mining operation.[84]

U.S.-based Freeport-McMoRan Copper & Gold Inc. is operating Grasberg, the world's largest open-pit gold mine. Profits from the operation have been the single biggest source of tax revenue for Indonesia. Land owned by the indigenous peoples, the Amungme and Kamoro, including a mountain sacred to them, was taken over without their consent by a 1967 agreement between Freeport and the Suharto regime. Not only have many villages been displaced, but mine wastes have been dumped on downstream tribal lands. In 1998, for example, some 200,000 tons of ore were dumped into the Ajkwa river system. These mine tailings have turned 230 square kilometers of the river delta into a lifeless wasteland.[85]

From the beginning, the local tribes opposed Freeport's presence, but this opposition was not linked to OPM's armed separatism until 1977. Indonesian security forces retaliated by bombing and burning villages. Freeport has maintained close ties with the armed forces, providing transportation, accommodation, and funding to the troops in return for military protection. Financial reports for the company suggest that it has made more than $9 million available to the military since the mid-1990s. Military reprisals not withstanding, land rights conflicts, compensation demands, human rights violations, and environmental damage keep triggering violent and nonviolent protests. And as in Aceh, the influx of Javanese migrants into West Papua has heightened tensions.[86]

Since 1998, pro-independence sentiments have strengthened due to two opposing factors: the greater political freedom of the post-Suharto era and the increasing military repression of separatist movements. The movement has grown to become a broad, civilian-based Papuan independence movement. But Jakarta dispatched thousands of additional troops after the Papuan Congress declared independence in June 2000. Civilians were attacked, peaceful protests banned, key Papuan leaders arrested, and access by journalists and human rights observers severely restricted. Papuan militants in turn have attacked military forces and non-Papuan migrants. Although the violence is currently less intense than in Aceh, the death toll since 1961 may be as high as 100,000.[87]

Under special autonomy packages, both West Papua and Aceh are to receive a larger share of the revenues derived from resources—80 percent of the income from mining and forestry industries, 30 percent from natural gas, and 15 percent from oil. But promises of autonomy have failed to satisfy the rebels, and these provinces are too valuable for the central government in Jakarta to grant full independence.[88]

BOUGAINVILLE: COPPER AND SECESSION

In Bougainville (an island that is part of Papua New Guinea), similar issues led to a decade-long war. The world's largest open-pit copper mine, owned jointly by·mining giant RTZ (80 percent) and the central government (20 percent), started operating at Panguna in 1972. But the severe social and environmental impacts of the mine reinforced demands for secession. (Bougainville was governed by Australia from 1920 until 1975, when it was subsumed into newly independent Papua New Guinea despite protests.) (See Figure 6.)[89]

Papua New Guinea's (PNG's) constitution declared that mineral rights belonged to the state, violating Bougainville traditions of land ownership and reinforcing the alienation of rule by a different ethnic group. Copper revenues of $500 million per year went to the central government and foreign investors, but the local population saw relatively few benefits. The presence of an affluent expatriate mining community and the influx of large numbers of workers from other parts of PNG (locals were paid considerably less than other workers) intensified Bougainvilleans' resentment of the mine. The mine also led to major social disruptions, including an unraveling of the island society's matriarchal structure. Mine tailings and chemical pollutants damaged about one-fifth the total land area, forcing village relocations, decimating food and cash crops like cocoa and bananas, contaminating rivers, and depleting fish stocks.[90]

Bougainvilleans' complaints and demands for adequate compensation were ignored. In 1988, they launched a campaign of sabotage that, spurred by human rights violations by government forces, quickly developed into guerrilla war. The mine fell to the rebels and was closed down in May 1989. The government reacted to this major loss of revenue by launching a series of ultimately futile military campaigns and a blockade of the island that led to the death of thousands of civilians. Government forces committed atrocities and burned thousands of homes, but failed to recapture the mine and withdrew in 1990. But as the 1990s progressed, tensions among Bougainville's different communities and language groups themselves broke out and led to violent conflict.[91]

Following defeat in one of the army's many attempts to recapture the island, in 1997 a desperate Julius Chan, PNG prime minister, offered $36 million in World Bank funds to the British mercenary firm Sandline International in a last-ditch effort to dislodge the Bougainville rebels. However, senior army officers—incensed that their own budget was being cut—forced Chan to cancel the Sandline contract and resign.[92]

Pressure mounted on both sides to end the war with growing realization of the horrendous costs of an unwinnable conflict. In 1998, a cease fire was signed and a small international peacekeeping force deployed. The conflict was formally ended in August 2001, following intense negotiations facilitated by New Zealand and Australia. The PNG parliament approved autonomy status for Bougainville in March 2002, with the prospect that a referendum on independence could be held in 10 to 15 years.[93]

NIGERIA: REPRESSION IN THE DELTA

Nigeria is one of the world's leading petroleum producers, and oil development has enriched a tiny minority of Nigerians and several foreign oil companies. But it has translated into

environmental devastation, health problems, and impoverishment for the inhabitants of the oil-producing areas that have
traditionally lived from fishing, cassava and other agricultural crops, and palm oil production. Oil industry jobs, meanwhile, are scarce. The Niger Delta, where oil production is
taking place, forms Africa's largest wetlands area, harboring
extensive mangrove forests and providing habitat for a number of unique plant and animal species. Poor industry practices,
such as constant flaring of natural gas, along with frequent oil
spills from antiquated pipelines and leaks from toxic waste pits,
have exacted a heavy toll on soil, vegetation, water, air, and
human health. Local communities complain of respiratory
problems, skin rashes, tumors, gastrointestinal problems, and
cancers. They have seen a drastic decline in the fish catch and
agricultural yields.[94]

Throughout the 1990s, local communities staged
protests, often directed against multinational oil companies
in Nigeria—primarily Royal Dutch/Shell as the largest producer, but also Chevron, Mobil, France's Elf, and Italy's Agip.
The Ogoni are one of the Niger Delta communities that
gained world attention for their cause. The Movement for the
Survival of the Ogoni People (MOSOP) organized mass
protests that succeeded in shutting down Shell operations in
Ogoni territory in 1993. The military dictatorship, which got
80 percent of its revenues from oil, responded with a campaign of violence and intimidation, and provoked various ethnic groups in the delta to attack each other. Some 2,000
Ogoni were killed and 80,000 uprooted; MOSOP leaders were
detained or forced to flee. In October 1995, the regime exe-
cuted Ken Saro-Wiwa, MOSOP's well-known spokesman, and
eight other leaders.[95]

Aided by weak enforcement policies and oppressive government, the oil companies have flaunted Nigeria's environmental laws and have largely evaded paying compensation for
damages to Delta communities. Corporate representatives
deny knowledge of the government's repressive tactics, but the
companies apparently often summon the notoriously abusive security forces to intervene against unarmed protesters.

Chevron helicopters were reportedly used in a 1998 assault against protesters. Elf and Agip are alleged to have instigated deadly attacks against, respectively, female protesters and a village that refused to let oil drilling go forward. Shell is reported to have helped finance and arm a local paramilitary force in Ogoniland. Exposed to increasingly unfavorable world opinion, Shell undertook a major review of its activities and attitudes toward Niger Delta communities. But as a 1999 Human Rights Watch report comments, the company's actual performance will ultimately be the test of whether this amounts to more than changed rhetoric.[96]

The death of military dictator Sani Abacha in June 1998 allowed a transition to an elected government in 1999. According to Human Rights Watch, this brought a "significant relaxation in the unprecedented repression...inflicted on the Nigerian people." A Human Rights Commission is investigating cases going as far back as 1965, and more than 10,000 petitions have been brought before it. Responding to claims brought against the Abacha dictatorship, the African Commission on Human and People's Rights, a unit of the Organization of African Unity (now the African Union), ruled that the Nigerian government should compensate the Ogoni for abuses they have suffered. Although western media attention has faded, protests and occupations of oil facilities surged after Abacha's death. The government withdrew the feared Internal Security Task Force from Ogoniland, but human rights abuses against those attempting to raise grievances in the oil-producing areas continue nevertheless. In this sense, at least, conditions in the delta have changed little. The central government has agreed to raise the share of oil revenues going to the delta from 3 to 13 percent, but only a portion has been paid out.[97]

While democratization efforts in Nigeria, Indonesia, and elsewhere give greater hope that these conflicts can be resolved, far more needs to happen to bolster the human and development rights of affected communities. Greater awareness and scrutiny are also needed in major consuming countries if the link between resources and repression is to be broken.

Collateral Damage:
The Environmental Toll

Many contemporary resource-related conflicts are being fought in areas of great environmental value. The Democratic Republic of the Congo, Indonesia, Papua New Guinea, and Colombia, for example, together account for 10 percent of the world's remaining intact forests. Not surprisingly, these and other countries in which resource conflicts are raging are home to some of the world's biodiversity hotspots. The Democratic Republic of the Congo, for example, accounts for more than half of Africa's forests. It has the largest number of bird and mammal species of any country on the continent (including okapis, rhinos, chimpanzees, and lowland gorillas) and is also one of the region's most flora-rich countries. Yet during the 1990s, Congo and other well-endowed countries suffered from the world's highest net loss of forest area.[98]

Mining and logging are highly destructive of the environment, both because of the methods of extraction used and because these operations often take place in ecologically fragile areas. This is particularly true of mining operations, which involve the removal of what the industry calls overburden—the soil and rock that obstruct access to desired ores. But along with this overburden, rich vegetation is removed as well, destroying or compromising the quality of natural habitat for many plants and animals. Moreover, mining companies use a range of toxic chemicals to treat the ores extracted. The resulting waste streams are often either intentionally dumped or leak accidentally, contaminating rivers and lakes. As for logging, it can in principle be done in relatively careful and responsible ways, but many timber operations still engage in devastating clear-cutting practices. The toll inflicted by large-scale logging includes soil erosion, more severe flooding, and the destruction of wildlife habitat and fisheries.[99]

These impacts are felt even under the best of circumstances. They are worse where resource extraction is done in a rapacious fashion that makes light of the survival interest of local communities and discounts biodiversity, as demonstrated in Aceh, West Papua, Bougainville, and many other locations. Kalimantan, the Indonesian part of the island of Borneo, for instance, is the scene of three decades of conflict between the indigenous population (more than 3 million people collectively known as the Dayak) on one hand, and loggers, palm oil plantation businesses, and plantation laborers on the other. The forests of Borneo are among the largest remaining tropical forests, but careless commercial logging has been rapidly eating into these areas since the 1960s. Only a small minority of logging companies, estimated at about 4 percent, follow ecological guidelines.[100]

A series of Indonesian laws passed in the 1960s marginalized the rights of indigenous peoples. The Basic Forestry Law of 1967 parcelled out huge chunks of Dayak forests to logging concessionaires (influential generals first, then timber companies headed by cronies of the Suharto military dictatorship). The Mining Law of 1968 similarly took control away from indigenous communities and overrode their traditional (and far less environmentally disrupting) ways of gold mining.[101]

The Suharto regime relied on foreign loans to pursue economic development. The loans were paid for by massive resource extraction, particularly timber. Foreign debt therefore translated into rapid deforestation. Almost 70 percent of Kalimantan's forests were opened to logging. In the province of Central Kalimantan alone, some 7 to 8 million hectares, an area larger than all of Ireland, were allocated to timber companies. The Indonesian government also invited oil palm companies to move in after forests had been cleared by loggers, and facilitated transmigration to provide cheap labor for the plantation companies. Although logging is destroying Borneo's forests at a rapid pace, some 63 percent of Kalimantan is still forested. But if current logging trends continue, the forests of West Kalimantan will be gone in 10 to 20 years.[102]

The enormous wealth that a small but politically well connected elite has derived from logging stands in stark contrast to the mortal threat that logging presents to the Dayak, whose livelihood—food, shelter, clothing, and medicine—is intimately connected to healthy forests. Borneo boasts a great variety of fish and birds, as well as rare species such as orangutans, bears, elephants, and rhinos. The Dayak have for centuries relied on agriculture, fishing, and hunting and gathering of forest products such as fruits, rattan, resins, oilseeds, and medicinal plants. But unsustainable logging has resulted in soil degradation, silted streams, diminished wildlife and biodiversity, greater droughts, and unprecedented floods affecting villages and croplands. The number of wild pigs and deer, which are an important Dayak food source, has fallen as habitats have shrunk. Freshwater fisheries have suffered from growing siltation and the depositing of chemicals used in timber and oil palm operations in rivers. Fish have declined in size, quantity, and variety.[103]

Under conditions of full-scale war, the consequences of rapacious resource extraction can be even more severe. Because much resource extraction occurs illegally, and because loggers and miners are intent on extracting resources before they might lose control over an area, they have no incentive to conduct their operations in a responsible, let alone truly sustainable, manner. Their primary interest is in raising funds for weapons purchases or self-enrichment and they try to extract as much, and as fast, as possible. In these circumstances, the enduring value of preserving biological treasure troves and ecosystems crucial to human wellbeing all too easily loses out to the urge to exploit the narrow spectrum of natural wealth—minerals, gemstones, and timber—that can be turned into cash.[104]

The eastern part of the Democratic Republic of the Congo has been ravaged by a series of civil wars and refugee flows since the early 1990s. Although it is impossible to assess the full consequences as long as war and insecurity prevail, there can be little doubt that a number of factors—the overall state of anarchy in much of the country, widespread illegal logging, mining, and poaching, resource battles, and refugee movements—have had a devastating impact on forests and wildlife.

The Rwandan civil war of 1990–94 spilled over into neighboring Zaïre almost from the beginning, with both sides conducting military operations in the Virungas area. The military presence in the forest kept growing, landmines were laid, and vegetation was cut down. But this was mere prelude to far greater destruction. Following the Rwandan genocide, nearly 2 million people left Rwanda in a sudden, massive out-flow in July 1994; half went to eastern Zaïre and settled mostly on the edge of Virunga Park or inside it. Desperate for firewood, the refugees cut and gathered as much as 1,000 tons of wood a day, causing serious deforestation. During the 27 months that the refugee camps existed, a total of 113 square kilometers of forestland was affected; of that, 75 square kilometers were clearcut.[105]

The subsequent Congolese civil wars (discussed earlier) imposed additional burdens. Congo's national parks—Kahuzi-Biega, Salonga, Virunga, Maiko, Garamba—and the Okapi Reserve have been severely affected by war, anarchy, refugee flows, and massive illegal resource extraction. (See Table 3, page 52.) But because no complete baseline wildlife or plant inventory had been conducted prior to the war, it is difficult to evaluate the full consequences.[106]

The lure of resource wealth drew not only a variety of armed factions into the Congo's natural parks, but also some 10,000 miners, with calamitous consequences. Kahuzi-Biega National Park and the Okapi Wildlife Reserve are both UNESCO World Heritage sites, a status that extols their unique value to all of humanity. But severe environmental degradation as a result of "gold rush"-like events has landed them on the organization's list of sites in danger. Poaching of elephant tusks left only 2 out of 350 elephant families in Kahuzi-Biega in 2000. Likewise, the number of eastern lowland gorillas has been so reduced that they are threatened with extinction. Coltan miners strip off the bark of eko trees to fashion troughs in which they flush out coltan from ore-bearing mud; thousands of trees have been destroyed, undermining the livelihoods of the local indigenous people, the Mbuti, who use the eko trees for gathering honey.[107]

Logging companies connected to Congolese rebel groups have engaged in rapacious clear-cutting operations. DARA-

TABLE 3

Impact of Armed Conflict on Protected Areas of the Democratic Republic of the Congo

Protected Area	Impact/Observation
Garamba National Park	One of the first protected areas affected by war. Meat poaching escalated when 80,000 Sudanese refugees settled along park's borders in 1991, and Sudanese rebel forces deployed nearby. During 1996–97 civil war in DRC, battles and looting took place inside the park. There were precipitous declines in mammal populations from 1995 to 1998: elephant population halved to less than 5,500, buffalos reduced one-third to fewer than 8,000. But poaching decreased after 1998.
Okapi Wildlife Reserve	Situated farther away from areas originally affected by civil war, the reserve was affected much later than other protected areas. Elephant poaching began only in 2000 (no appreciable decline in population found), and number of illegal coltan and gold mines increased significantly the same year.
Kahuzi-Biega National Park	Has suffered since first influx of Rwandan refugees in 1994. Rwandan Interahamwe forces (which carried out the Rwandan genocide) and Congolese (Mayi-Mayi) rebels control lowland portion of the park (encompassing 90 percent of the total territory), where they are involved in gold, castorite, and coltan mining and ivory poaching. Elephant population nearly destroyed, down from 350 families to 2. Lowland gorilla population halved (down to 130), though due more to conditions of anarchy than acts of war per se.
Virungas National Park	Rwandan refugees that include heavily-armed former government soldiers engage in poaching of antelopes, forest buffalos, and elephants that are subsequently sold through illegal commercial networks established by Zaïrian soldiers. In late 1996, Congolese Mayi-Mayi militias decimated hippopotamuses that remained along the Rutshuri and Rwindi rivers, and ADFL (anti-Mobutu) rebels slaughtered antelope and buffalo populations. In 1999, Rwandan-allied rebels (RCD-Goma) killed at least 330 buffalo and 450 antelope, though a large portion of the mountain gorilla population apparently continued to survive.
Salonga National Park	Has been a poacher's paradise for more than two decades, long preceding the current armed conflicts. Lies in territory controlled by government forces in west-central Congo. Poachers now include heavily-armed deserters from former dictator Mobutu's army. Elephant populations severely reduced.

Table 3 (continued)

Maiko National Park	Has been a battleground during the civil war that started in 1998; government soldiers and other armed groups involved in poaching and illegal mining.

Source: See Endnote 106.

Forest Company, for example, had been denied a logging license by the government in early 1998, but obtained a concession in Orientale Province in 2000 from RCD-ML, a rebel faction allied with Uganda. It subsequently carried out logging "without consideration of any of the minimum acceptable rules of timber harvesting for sustainable forest management," according to a UN expert panel. Satellite images show deforestation taking place at an alarming rate. Although DARA-Forest failed to satisfy Forest Stewardship Council procedures and evaded international requirements for timber certification, the UN panel found that companies from Belgium, Denmark, Switzerland, China, Japan, Kenya, and the United States nevertheless imported the company's timber via Uganda.[108]

Impacts similar to those seen in the Congo have been felt in other war zones. In Sierra Leone, government soldiers, RUF rebels, and militia forces spent long periods in forest reserve areas at various times during the conflict. Armed groups relied on monkeys and bush animals for food. The general breakdown of order led to serious encroachment on the Western Area Peninsula Forest, located on Freetown peninsula, and substantial deforestation due to indiscriminate logging. Illegal logging abounded throughout the country during the civil war.[109]

Neighboring Liberia still has a considerable amount of its original rainforest cover and a rich array of plant and animal species, including forest elephants and the endangered Pygmy hippopotamus. But the scale of timber cutting now is such that its forests are likely to be denuded in little more than a decade; according to current plans, the pace is actually set to intensify further. Responsible forest management and replanting efforts are virtually unknown. Global Witness observes that "inexperienced...chainsaw operators harvest trees; species of trees that are harvested but not in demand are left behind to rot in the bush camps. Harvesting of undersized logs is rampant, 'clearfelling' is widely practised...."[110]

Sanctions, Certification Systems, and Economic Diversification

Resource-related conflicts have been raging in large part because of a business-as-usual approach by governments and corporations. But prodded by NGOs, the situation is beginning to change.

Confronted with severe conflicts in Sierra Leone, Angola, and Congo, the UN Security Council has increasingly examined the role of resources in perpetuating these wars. It imposed a number of embargoes on the illicit diamond trade and on the purchases of arms, equipment, and fuel paid for with diamond money. (See Table 4.) The diamond embargo on Liberia, for example, has had some success, contributing to a dramatic decline in Liberian-based diamond smuggling. Nonetheless, these efforts are only a beginning. Observers from NGOs and expert UN panels have called for similar measures that would cover additional types of resources. But governments have blocked action in some cases; for instance, France and China, the two leading importers of timber from Liberia, opposed UN sanctions against Liberian timber exports.[111]

It has also become painfully obvious that existing sanctions are being violated by unscrupulous commodities producers, traders, bankers, and governments. There is an urgent need to step up international efforts to monitor compliance with sanctions and to improve the capacity to enforce embargoes and investigate violations so that traffickers can no longer operate with impunity.[112]

Growing energy is being directed toward efforts to make it more difficult for resources gained through conflict to be sold on world markets. By far the most attention has gone to the

TABLE 4

Resource Conflicts and United Nations Sanctions

Resolution	Date	Security Council Action
788	November 1992	Arms embargo against Liberia.
792	December 1992	Ban against exports of round logs from Cambodia (directed against the financial basis of the Khmer Rouge rebels).
864	September 1993	Embargo on deliveries of arms, military equipment, and fuel to Angola's UNITA rebels after their rejection of the 1992 election results.
1127	August 1997	Additional sanctions against UNITA (freezing of bank accounts; prohibiting foreign travel by senior UNITA personnel; closing of UNITA offices abroad).
1132	October 1997	Embargo on arms and oil supplies to Sierra Leone; travel ban on members of military junta (oil embargo terminated in March 1998).
1171	June 1998	Arms embargo and travel ban on anti-government forces in Sierra Leone.
1173	June 1998	Embargo on direct and indirect import of Angolan diamonds not approved under an Angolan government certificate of origin regime.
1237	May 1999	Established a panel to investigate violations of sanctions against UNITA.
1306	July 2000	Embargo on direct and indirect import of all rough diamonds from Sierra Leone. Following the establishment of a new monitoring regime, the embargo was narrowed to non-official exports in October 2000.
1343	March 2001	Demands that Liberia cease financial and military support for RUF, and cease imports of Sierra Leonean rough diamonds that do not have an official certificate of origin; embargo on arms deliveries to Liberia and travel ban against its political and military leaders (extended for another year in May 2002); embargo against Liberian diamond exports threatened unless Liberia can show that it is not supporting RUF.

Source: See Endnote 111.

diamond industry. The governments of Sierra Leone, Angola, and the Democratic Republic of the Congo are backing schemes under which only diamonds with proper documentation are considered legal. All gems are to be accompanied by certificates of origin, whose digital "fingerprint" is shared with authorities in importing countries. While polished diamonds cannot be traced to their origin, a recent technological breakthrough allows some high-tech sleuthing to pinpoint the source of rough stones by comparing trace amounts of impurities in the diamonds.[113]

But a certificate-of-origin system can be undermined by poor enforcement and circumvented by intricate international smuggling networks. For example, a UN report in October 2001 found that $1 million worth of diamonds were still being smuggled out of Angola every day. Lax government controls in the major diamond trading and cutting centers (Belgium, Switzerland, the United Kingdom, Israel, and others) and the opaque, unaccountable nature of the diamond industry have also been major obstacles in the struggle to root out conflict diamonds. A March 2000 UN investigative report on how sanctions against UNITA were circumvented concluded that Belgian authorities "failed to establish an effective import identification regime" or to effectively "monitor the activities of suspect brokers, dealers, and traders."[114]

The Belgian and British governments have since expressed their determination to crack down on conflict diamonds, and the Belgian government imposed strict controls on them in 2001. Also, the Belgian Senate established a commission of inquiry in November 2001 to investigate the involvement of Belgian and foreign companies in illegal resource exploitation in the Democratic Republic of the Congo. The Antwerp-based Diamond High Council has been working with the governments of Sierra Leone, Angola, Democratic Republic of the Congo, Côte d'Ivoire, and Guinea to develop tamper-proof certification systems for diamond exports. Efforts are also continuing in the United States, the world's largest importer of diamonds, to ban imports of illegally mined diamonds. Legislation was introduced in both chambers of the U.S. Congress;

of the two bills, the Senate version is considerably stronger.[115]

In recognition of the ease with which country-by-country diamond certification schemes and national customs regulations can be evaded, support has been growing for establishing a standardized global certification scheme. Since May 2000, representatives from 37 nations, the diamond industry, and a number of NGOs have conducted negotiations (referred to as the Kimberley Process, after the town in South Africa where the first meeting was held) to develop an international system. In March 2002, delegations reached agreement on a range of issues, including establishment of a database and standards for handling rough diamonds at each successive stage, from the mine to where they are cut and polished. Final details of the plan are to be considered in November 2002.[116]

But as Ian Smillie of the Partnership Africa Canada points out, participating governments rejected a critical element, namely independent, effective monitoring of the regulations and control mechanisms that each nation is supposed to put in place so that a global system can go into effect. Currently, very few countries have adequate measures in place. National capabilities and political will differ widely, and a tough-minded review will be essential to ensure that the policies adopted by all governments are up to the task. Otherwise, existing loopholes will simply be codified.[117]

Although the Kimberley Process scheme is a step forward, the March 2002 draft has a number of critical shortcomings. It relies primarily on voluntary participation and adherence by governments and industry, and lacks an international authority to monitor and enforce rules. The draft proposal entails recommendations, rather than binding controls, for how diamonds are to be handled from the time they are mined to the time they are first exported. Participation in the "chain of warranties" that follows the initial export (as diamonds are sold and resold, polished, and incorporated into jewelry) is to be voluntary, and monitoring and enforcement are left to self-regulation. Further, it is unclear how existing stockpiles with undocumented sources will be handled, and there is a danger that conflict diamonds could simply be declared as stockpiles when the scheme is initiated. Although progress has been made on relevant data to be shared, steps toward improving and standardizing data remain to be spelled out; it remains to be decided who will compile statistics and analyze them, and how results will be reported. All in all, there is considerable doubt that the provisions in the current draft will be effective in countering conflict diamonds.[118]

Effective measures will be needed for other conflict resources as well. For instance, there are no international rules or agreements that could presently address the issue of illegal logging and conflict timber. The UN Forum on Forests, for instance, does not have a specific mandate for such a purpose, though it could prove a useful forum for international discussion. A certification system might build on existing efforts by the Forest Stewardship Council to ascertain whether timber is being produced in a sustainable manner. The Council effort, initiated in 1993, entails independent audits to verify compliance with a series of requirements. Of particular interest is its chain-of-custody certification, which seeks to trace the lumber or furniture on consumer store shelves all the way back to the forest where the trees were felled. This is the kind of tracing and accounting that would be needed to determine whether timber had been produced in conflict situations.[119]

It is clear that a number of businesses—oil and mining companies, trading firms, airlines and shipping companies, manufacturers, and banks—carry a degree of responsibility for the events that have triggered campaigns against blood diamonds and other conflict resources. This responsibility ranges from an active role (in which companies are directly and knowingly involved in illicit resource exploitation), to a silent complicity (in which firms do business with repressive regimes because of lucrative contracts), to a passive enabling role (in which few questions are asked by companies down the supply chain about the origin of raw materials or about money being laundered).

International embargoes and UN reports have begun to create greater transparency. NGO campaigns have tugged at the cloak of complicity through investigative reports and by "naming and shaming" specific corporations, in an effort to compel them to do business more ethically or to terminate their operations in certain locations. Such campaigns have been most potent in the case of companies that sell highly visible consumer products or whose corporate logos and slogans are familiar to millions.[120]

At the end of the 1990s, the diamond industry was hit by a wave of bad publicity and faced the threat of consumer boycotts. De Beers, the industry's monopolist, was sufficiently embarrassed by London-based NGO Global Witness, which revealed that the company had knowingly purchased diamonds from Angola's UNITA rebels, that it decided to adopt a more responsible policy, urging the rest of the industry to follow suit. Similarly, when the role of coltan in the Congo war become more widely known, consumer electronics companies scrambled to avoid the kind of negative publicity that the diamond industry had endured. Companies like Ericsson, Nokia, Motorola, Compaq, and Intel suddenly scrutinized their supply chains and put pressure on mineral processing firms to stop purchasing illegally mined coltan. Kemet and Cabot, U.S. companies processing coltan, cancelled orders for ores originating from the Democratic Republic of the Congo, and Belgium's Sogem (a subsidiary of Umicore) terminated its partnership with a Congolese coltan supplier. The Belgian airline Sabena stopped its coltan shipments from Rwanda to Europe. A number of oil companies have also been subjected to growing scrutiny. The threat of potentially losing access to the U.S. market—following proposals to bar companies invested in Sudanese oil production—convinced Canadian company Talisman to sell its stake in Sudanese oil projects to India's Oil and Natural Gas Corporation.[121]

Still, many unscrupulous companies are ready to step into the void, and continued international scrutiny is essential. In place of Sabena, for instance, the Dutch carrier Martinair is now flying coltan from Kigali into Amsterdam. In the case of diamonds, a network of Israeli businessmen has taken advantage of De Beer's exit from dealing in conflict gems, paying for diamonds with money, arms, and military training.[122]

On a different front, lawsuits have been filed in the United States against a number of corporations, arguing that these companies have colluded with various governments in human rights violations aimed at suppressing opposition to a variety of resource extraction projects. Among the defendants are Shell (concerning events in Nigeria's Ogoniland), Rio Tinto (Bougainville), ExxonMobil (Aceh), and Unocal (Burma). Via the State Department, the Bush administration has requested that the Bougainville and Aceh suits be dismissed (the Bougainville case was subsequently thrown out in March 2002, whereas a decision on the Aceh case is still pending as of this writing); the administration has yet to comment on the Burma case.[123]

Where development aid and private investments continue to flow into the extractive sector, they should go only to governments that are democratic and accountable to their own citizens. A new initiative (simply called "Publish What You Pay") by philanthropist George Soros and a large coalition of NGOs from developed and developing countries proposes that natural resource companies be required, as a condition of being listed on leading stock exchanges and financial markets, to disclose all taxes, fees, royalties, and other payments they make to host governments. Such a step would shed some light on often opaque financial transfers, and increase accountability of how such payments are used. The initiative states that "mining, gas, and oil companies cannot control how governments spend taxes, royalties, and fees. But they do have a responsibility to disclose the payments they make so citizens can hold their governments accountable. Companies that fail to do so are complicit in the disempowerment of the people of the countries to which the resources belong."[124]

Ensuring that the flow of resource income benefits the public good instead of feeding corruption, funding repression, and fueling conflict remains a tremendous challenge. A recent accord between the World Bank and the host governments concerning construction of an oil pipeline from Doba in southern Chad to Cameroon's Atlantic coast attempted to establish mechanisms that have just this aim. (The accord was in part a response to a scandal in 2000, when Chad's government secretly bought weapons with a portion of $25 million received in oil "bonuses" paid by ExxonMobil, Chevron, and Petronas. These arms were used to suppress a revolt in the Doba region, where oil production is to start in 2003, leading to hundreds of deaths.) A formula was agreed upon that allocates 80 percent of incoming funds to education, health, social services, rural development, infrastructure, and environmental needs. Under the complex arrangement, oil revenues (as much as $5 billion over the next quarter-century) are to be initially deposited in an escrow account. The escrow account is to be audited independently and the entire process supervised by a control and monitoring board composed of government officials and representatives of labor, human rights, and other groups.[125]

Reality, however, appears to tell a different story. Local and international NGOs, as well as an independent inspection panel of the World Bank, point to evidence that oversight mechanisms have not been allowed to function as planned, environmental problems (water depletion and pollution, illegal logging, and poaching) are inadequately addressed, protection measures for local indigenous communities have not been carried out, labor legislation is not being respected, and democratic principles and human rights are being violated. The lesson from this experience is that much work remains to be done to translate principles from paper into reality, and that governments, corporations, and international donors will not do so in the absence of pressure from watchdog groups and informed public opinion. The "resource curse" is not an easily cured affliction.[126]

There is growing awareness that natural resources will continue to fuel deadly conflicts as long as consumer societies import and use materials irrespective of where they originate and under what conditions they were produced. Support is growing for the idea that companies need to adopt more ethical ways of doing business. Shareholder activism and campaigns for ethical investing can help achieve these goals. But it is clear that activities to date are only a beginning. Governments and international organizations will need to work hard to create greater corporate transparency. So far, western nations have been all too ready to turn a blind eye in order to protect the interests of their own corporations.[127]

Another priority area for action concerns the massive proliferation of small arms. As awareness of the impact of small arms in resource-related conflicts and other settings has grown, national governments, regional organizations, and the United Nations have become more active in seeking ways to check the spread of these weapons, particularly illegal transfers. Especially noteworthy is a moratorium on the trade and manufacture of such weapons in West Africa, which was signed in October 1998 and renewed for another three years in 2001. Also, a UN-assisted effort is being made to collect weapons already in circulation, but West Africa remains a region awash in small arms.[128]

The small arms plague can be tackled successfully only with broad international cooperation and sustained effort. A UN conference on small arms was held in July 2001, with the expectation of launching efforts to conclude international agreements on marking and tracing weapons, regulating arms brokers, and establishing stricter export criteria. The opposition of a few governments, most notably the United States, nearly derailed the conference, however. The Bush administration opposed a number of measures, including restrictions on civilian ownership of such weapons, prohibitions against sales to nongovernmental entities such as rebel forces, and any limitations on the legal trade. Although the conference outcome was a low-common-denominator action program, it nevertheless provides a basis for stepped-up efforts to pursue post-conflict small arms disarmament, to destroy surplus and illegal arms, to demobilize soldiers and reintegrate them into civil society, and, most important, to improve transparency and greater knowledge about transfers.[129]

Experience to date also provides a strong case for improving peacekeeping capabilities. The conflicts in Angola and Sierra Leone have attracted two of the largest UN peacekeeping efforts. There is also a small peacekeeping force in the

Congo; the UN may be asked to verify the disarmament and demobilization of rebel forces that is envisioned in a July 2002 agreement between the government and Rwanda.[130]

But UN efforts confront a number of severe handicaps in such conflicts. The first concerns the warring parties. They may agree to cease-fires or even peace agreements as an expedient move that allows them to maneuver for advantage, only to return to violence at an opportune moment.

There are also systemic weaknesses in UN peacekeeping. Since there is no standing peacekeeping force, the United Nations relies on national governments to make personnel and equipment available. Typically, it takes several months for a mission to reach its authorized deployment strength. The numbers of peacekeepers are often inadequate to the task, and many of them are ill equipped and poorly trained. National contingents frequently do not work together well and sometimes fail to adhere to the mission's mandate.[131]

Fixing the deficiencies inherent in the current approach to peacekeeping would not only help brighten the chances of success in ending ongoing resource-based conflicts, it could also constitute something of a deterrent to future resource looters. An effective peacekeeping system that deploys well-trained and well-equipped troops in a timely fashion and that is able to protect victims (instead of adopting a false neutrality) would make a significant difference. An effective system would provide capacities to intercept smuggling routes, enforce peace agreements, and facilitate disarmament and demobilization of combatants. To establish such a system, governments must be prepared to invest adequate money, effort, and political support.

The policies discussed here are largely concerned with reacting to resource-based conflict rather than preventing it. Prevention is not an easy task, and there is no silver bullet. Promoting democratization, justice, and greater respect for human rights are key tasks, along with efforts to reduce the impunity with which some governments and rebel groups engage in extreme violence. Another challenge is to facilitate the diversification of the economy away from a strong dependence on primary commodities to a broader mix of activities. A more diversified economy would provide better economic balance, reduce vulnerability to the "resource curse," and lessen the likelihood that natural resources become pawns in a struggle among ruthless contenders for wealth and power.

Investing in human development, improving health and education services, and providing adequate jobs and opportunities for social and economic advancement will go a long way toward reducing the risk that a country's natural resource endowment will become its undoing. This is an investment that needs to be made not only by the governments concerned but also by the World Bank and other multilateral development agencies that have generously funded oil, mining, and logging projects. It must also be a priority for the rich nations that have for so long benefited from cheap raw material supplies while turning a blind eye to the destruction at their source.

Appendices

Where Resources and Conflict Intersect: Selected Examples

Location –Resource	Observation
Sudan –Oil	Civil war between North and South re-started in 1983 (Khartoum reneged on a peace pact after oil was discovered in 1980), resulting in more than 2 million deaths, 1 million refugees, and 4.5 million displaced. Oil revenues of $400 million per year helped triple military expenditures and increase arms imports. (Oil also facilitates domestic arms production: under a January 2002 agreement, Russia will help develop oil fields while Sudan will purchase Russian arms and assemble Russian-designed battle tanks.) To keep paying for the war, the government must expand oil production, which means exploiting oil deposits deeper in rebel-held territory (the South holds 75 percent of known oil reserves). To depopulate and control oil-producing and potentially oil-rich areas, government forces are conducting a "scorched earth" policy (aerial bombing of villages, destroying harvests, looting livestock, blocking humanitarian aid deliveries), and are fomenting inter-tribal warfare by supplying arms to some factions. SPLA (Sudan People's Liberation Army) opposition forces have targeted oil installations, and are also acquiring more sophisticated weapons. More intense and deadly battles have ensued, leading to massive displacement of civilians and food insecurity. But the SPLA has been unable to stop the flow of oil and may lose ground. Under growing international pressure, the two sides have entered negotiations to end the conflict.
Afghanistan –Emeralds –Lapis lazuli –Opium	During the 1980s war against Soviet occupation and the 1990s civil war, the Mujaheddin warlords used drug money to help fund their military campaigns and line their own pockets. Convoys carrying weapons into Afghanistan via the covert supply line organized by the U.S. and Pakistani intelligence agencies carried opium on the way out. From 10 tons per year prior to the 1979 Soviet invasion, the Afghan opium harvest grew to 1,200 tons in 1989 and double that in the early 1990s. After the Taliban conquest in the mid-1990s, production nearly doubled again, peaking at 4,600 tons in 1999, or 70 percent of the world's supply. The Taliban imposed a 10 percent tax on poppy growers and a 20 percent tax on opium traders, reaping $40 million to $50 million per year. Following severe international criticism, Taliban leader Mul-

66 THE ANATOMY OF RESOURCE WARS

lah Omar issued a decree in July 2000 banning the cultivation (but not the sale) of opium. Existing stockpiles of 220 tons were not affected, but the decree led to a 96 percent reduction in opium production. The ban was rescinded in the aftermath of September 11, 2001. Prior to the Taliban's ouster, warlords of the opposition Northern Alliance financed their military operations through the sale of emeralds and lapis lazuli (an azure-blue semiprecious stone), earning up to $60 million per year. But they also profited from selling opium and its by-products.

Cambodia
 – Sapphires
 – Rubies
 – Timber

Following the end of Chinese aid in 1989, the Khmer Rouge resorted to resource looting to finance their operations. Mining and logging licenses granted to Thai companies in Khmer Rouge territory (rich in rubies, sapphires, and timber) earned the group as much as $240 million a year in the early- to mid-1990s. Gem depletion and Thai government restrictions on the timber trade across the border caused a sharp income drop after 1995. Along with key defections in 1996, this severely weakened the Khmer Rouge.

The Cambodian government was making some $100-150 million a year in the mid-1990s from secret, illicit deals giving Vietnamese loggers access to timber concessions (enriching military leaders). But extensive deforestation cut earnings in later years, and much was pocketed by timber barons and corrupt politicians. Rivalry between the two parties in the government coalition (Funcinpec led by Prince Ranariddh and the CPP led by Hun Sen) led each side to try and build the strength of portions of the armed forces loyal to it with the help of timber money. The CPP coup d'etat against Funcinpec in July 1997 was supported by timber tycoons and regional military commanders in return for carte blanche logging rights. But as regional military units turned into de facto warlords and possible rivals to the central government, Hun Sen cracked down on illegal logging in 1999. Severe deforestation led to unprecedented flooding in 2000, ruining rice crops and causing massive displacements of people.

Burma
 – Timber
 – Opium
 – Precious
   stones
 – Natural
   gas

"Teak wars" between the government and a variety of ethnic insurgencies over control of forests on the border with Thailand propelled the rate of deforestation in Burma to third-highest in the world in the 1990s. Through logging deals with Thailand, the military regime earned at least $112 million per year, and logging roads opened up once inaccessible areas for the Burmese army, facilitating the supply of frontline troops and attacks against rebels from the Mon minority. Revenues from the sale of hardwoods logged by Chinese and Malaysian companies in northern Burma have gone toward weapons purchases from China and Russia. Timber also provides insurgent groups with revenues, through Thai logging companies operating in rebel-controlled areas. But the Burmese government was also able to reach agreements with two groups, the Shan State Army (1989) and the Kachin Independence Army (1994), under which they jointly exploited opium, timber, and precious stones in rebel-held territory.

The military junta also earns revenues from offshore natural gas reserves in the Andaman Sea. Unocal and Total built a pipeline to Thailand through the Tenasserim region, the last primary rainforest on mainland Asia and a biodiversity hotspot. The area is home to rebellious Mon and Karen ethnic minorities. Completed in 1999, the pipeline was constructed with forced labor. Government soldiers killed and tortured people from local communities, forced forest dwellers to resettle, and killed rhinoceros, elephants, and other wild animals. The pipeline has led to ongoing, unchecked logging in the region.

Source: See endnote 4.

APPENDIX 2

Sources of Information on Conflict Commodities and Related Issues

Amnesty International
International Secretariat
1 Easton Street
London WC1X 0DW
United Kingdom
e-mail: amnestyis@amnesty.org
website: www.amnesty.org
Leading international human rights organization. Also runs a "True Cost of Diamonds" Campaign (website: web.amnesty.org/diamonds/index.html).

Campaign to Eliminate Conflict Diamonds
c/o Physicians for Human Rights, Washington Office
1156 15th Street, NW #1001
Washington, DC 20005
tel: (202) 728-5335
fax: (202) 728-3053
e-mail: phrusa@phrusa.org

website: www.phrusa.org/campaigns/sierra_leone/conflict_diamonds.html
The Campaign is a coalition of North American human rights, religious, humanitarian, peace, and development groups committed to ending the trade in "conflict diamonds" and supporting human rights in diamond-producing countries in Africa.

Christian Aid
35 Lower Marsh
Waterloo, London SE1 7RL
United Kingdom
tel.: +44 (020) 7620 4444
fax: +44 (020) 7620 0719
e-mail: info@christian-aid.org
website: www.christian-aid.org.uk
An agency of the churches in the United Kingdom and Ireland,

Christian Aid works to end poverty
and to change the rules that keep
people poor.

CorpWatch
PO Box 29344
San Francisco, CA 94129
tel: 415-561-6568
fax: 415-561-6493
e-mail: corpwatch@corpwatch.org
website: www.corpwatch.org
CorpWatch works to foster democratic control over corporations by
building grassroots globalization—a
diverse movement for human
rights, labor rights and
environmental justice.

Earth Rights
U.S. Office:
1612 K St. NW, Suite 401
Washington, DC 20006
tel.: 202-466-5188
fax: 202-466-5189
e-mail: infousa@earthrights.org

Southeast Asia Office:
P.O. Box 123
Chiang Mai University
Chiang Mai, 50202
Thailand
tel: +66 (1) 531-1256
e-mail: infoasia@earthrights.org
website: www.earthrights.org
Documenting human rights and
environmental abuses with focus
on Southeast Asia; working to hold
corporations accountable for fair
human rights, labor, and environmental practices (including litiga-
tion in U.S. courts).

Fatal Transactions Campaign
c/o Netherlands Institute for
   Southern Africa
P.O.Box 10707
1001 ES Amsterdam
Netherlands
tel.: (20) 520 6210
fax: (20) 520 6249

e-mail: ft@niza.nl
website: www.niza.nl/fataltransactio
ns/index.html
A coalition of European nongovernmental organizations
campaigning against conflict
diamonds.

Fafo Institute for Applied Social
   Science
Programme for International Co-
operation and Conflict Resolution
Borggata 2b, P.O. Box 2947 Tøyen
0608 Oslo
Norway
tel.: +47 (22) 08 86 00
fax: +47 (22) 08 87 00
e-mail: pisk@fafo.no
website: www.fafo.no/piccr
Publishes a series of research reports
on "Economies of Conflict."

Global Policy Forum
777 United Nations Plaza, Suite 7G
New York, NY 10017
tel.: 212-557-3161
fax: 212-557-3165
e-mail: globalpolicy@globalpolicy.org
website: www.globalpolicy.org
Maintains extensive online collection of articles and documents on
conflict commodities:
"Diamonds in Conflict": www.globa
lpolicy.org/security/issues/diamond
/index.htm
"The Dark Side of Natural Resources":
www.globalpolicy.org/security/docs
/minindx.htm

Global Witness
PO Box 6042
London, N19 5WP
United Kingdom
tel: (020) 7272 6731
fax: +44 (020) 7272 9425
e-mail: mail@globalwitness.org
website: www.globalwitness.org
Global Witness aims to break the
links between resources and conflict

by changing corporate and government practices that result in unregulated resource exploitation. It has documented the exploitation of timber, oil, and diamond resources in countries such as Cambodia, Angola, Liberia, and the Democratic Republic of the Congo.

Human Rights Watch
350 Fifth Avenue
New York, NY 10118
tel: 212-290-4700
fax: 212-736-1300
e-mail: hrwnyc@hrw.org
website: www.hrw.org
Leading human rights organization; publishes extensive country reports.

International Crisis Group
Headquarters:
149 Avenue Louise, Level 24
1050 Brussels
Belgium
tel: +32 (2) 502 90 38;
fax: +32 (2) 502 50 38
e-mail: icgbrussels@crisisweb.org
website: www.crisisweb.org

Washington Office:
1522 K Street, Suite 200
Washington, DC 20005
tel: 202-408-8012
fax: 202-408-8258
e-mail: icgwashington@crisisweb.org
Working to strengthen the capacity of the international community to anticipate, understand and act to prevent and contain conflict, through reports based on field research.

International Peace Academy
777 United Nations Plaza
New York, NY 10017
tel.: +1 (212) 687-4300
fax: +1 (212) 983-8246
e-mail: ipa@ipacademy.org
website: www.ipacademy.org/Program
s/Research/ProgReseEcon_body.htm

Conducting a 3-year research and policy project on "Economic Agendas in Civil Wars."

International Peace Information Service
Italiëlei 98a
2000 Antwerp
Belgium
tel: +32 (3) 225 0022
fax: +32 (3) 231 0151
e-mail: ipis@glo.be
website:
users.skynet.be/ipis/mainuk.htm
IPIS is an independent study and information service; partner in the Human Security and the International Diamond Trade in Africa program; research on conflict diamonds, mining and conflict, mercenaries and private security companies.

Oxfam America
26 West Street
Boston, MA 02111
tel.: 1-800-77-Oxfamusa
fax: 617-728-2594
e-mail: info@oxfamamerica.org
website: www.oxfamamerica.org
Currently runs campaigns on conflict diamonds in Africa and on oil, gas, and mining issues related to poverty and health.

Partnership Africa Canada
323 Chapel Street
Ottawa, Ontario K1N 7Z2
Canada
tel: 613-237-6768
fax: 613-237-6530
e-mail:
hsda@partnershipafricacanada.org
website: partnershipafricacanada.or
g/hsdp/index.html
PAC, in collaboration with the International Peace Information Service in Belgium and the Network Movement for Justice and Develop-

ment in Sierra Leone, launched
the Human Security and the
International Diamond Trade in
Africa program in January 2001.

Project Underground
1916A MLK Jr. Way
Berkeley, CA 94704
tel.: 510-705-8981
fax: 510-705-8983
e-mail:
project_underground@moles.org
website: www.moles.org
Project Underground publishes
reports on the environmental and
human rights abuses committed by
resource extraction companies and
seeks to assist affected communities
in their efforts to achieve economic
and environmental justice.

Rainforest Action Network
221 Pine St., Suite 500
San Francisco, CA 94104
tel: 415-398-4404
fax: 415-398-2732
e-mail: rainforest@ran.org
website: www.ran.org and
www.rainforestweb.org
Rainforest Action Network works to
protect the Earth's rainforests and
support the rights of their inhabitants through education, grassroots
organizing, and nonviolent direct
action. One specific campaign has
been in support of the U'wa indigenous population of Colombia.
website: www.ran.org/ran_campaig
ns/beyond_oil/oxy/

Small Arms Survey
Graduate Institute of International
   Studies, Geneva
12, Avenue de Sécheron
1202 Geneva
Switzerland
tel. (22) 908 57 77
fax: +41 (22) 732 27 38
e-mail: smallarm@hei.unige.ch

website: www.smallarmssurvey.org
Principal source of impartial and
public information on small arms
and light weapons, and nexus for
international network of researchers
and NGOs working on small arms
issues; publishes annual Small Arms
Survey.

United Nations
Headquarters, New York

Department of Peacekeeping
   Operations:
website: www.un.org/Depts/dpko/dp
ko/home_bottom.htm

Department of Political Affairs,
Security Council Affairs Division:
Conflict Diamonds Web page:
www.un.org/peace/africa/Diamond
.html

Security Council:
Council resolutions and other documents available online at:
www.un.org/Docs/sc/

World Bank
Project on "The Economics of Civil
War, Crime, and Violence"
under the direction of Paul Collier,
Research Director, Development
Economics Research Group
(DECRG), and Ibrahim Elbadawi,
Africa Department, World Bank
website: econ.worldbank.org/progr
ams/conflict and
www.worldbank.org/research/conflict/

Notes

1.   Rachel L. Swarns, "War-Weary Angola Meets New Challenge: Peace," *New York Times*, 28 April 2002; Rachel L. Swarns, "Angola's Fragile Peace Rests on a New Guerrilla Leader," *New York Times*, 10 April 2002.

2.   UNICEF quoted by Holger Jensen, "Spoils of War," *Nando Times*, 15 March 2000; Global Witness, *A Crude Awakening* (London: 1999), p. 4; United Nations Development Programme (UNDP), *Human Development Report 2001* (New York: Oxford University Press, 2001), Annex Tables 1, 4, 9; UNDP, *Human Development Report 2002* (New York: Oxford University Press, 2002).

3.   Displaced population and food aid dependence from Blaine Harden, "Africa's Gems: Warfare's Best Friend," *New York Times*, 6 April 2000, and from Fatal Transactions Campaign, "Diamond, a Merciless Beauty," <www.niza.nl/uk/campaigns/diamonds>, viewed 5 July 2001.

4.   Appendix 1 is based on the following sources: **Sudan** from Christian Aid, *Scorched Earth* (London: 2001); from Dan Connell, "Sudan: Recasting U.S. Policy," *Foreign Policy in Focus*, August 2001; from Amnesty International, "Oil in Sudan—Deteriorating Human Rights," 3 May 2000; from International Crisis Group, *Dialogue or Destruction? Organizing for Peace as the War in Sudan Escalates*, ICG Africa Report No. 48, Nairobi and Brussels, 27 June 2002; from Elisabeth Sköns et al., "Military Expenditure and Arms Production," in Stockholm International Peace Research Institute (SIPRI), *SIPRI Yearbook 2001: Armaments, Disarmament and International Security* (New York: Oxford University Press, 2001), p. 278; from Small Arms Survey, *Small Arms Survey 2002* (New York: Oxford University Press, 2002), p. 142; from Human Rights Watch, "Sudan: Human Rights Developments," *Human Rights Watch World Report 2001* (New York: 2001), p. 5; from Sudan Update, "Raising the Stakes: Oil and Conflict in Sudan," <www.sudanupdate.org/REPORTS/OIL/21 oc.html>, from Stratfor, "Sudan and Russia Forging New Ties Around Oil and Arms," re-posted on Global Policy Forum Web site, <www.globalpolicy.org/security/natres/oil/su dan/2002/0122arms.htm>; and from "On Sudan's Horizon, Maybe Congo's," *The Economist*, 25 July 2002. **Afghanistan** from Ahmed Rashid, *Taliban: Militant Islam, Oil and Fundamentalism in Central Asia* (New Haven: Yale University Press, 2000); from John K. Cooley, *Unholy Wars: Afghanistan, America and International Terrorism* (London, Pluto Press, 2000); from Reyko Huang, "Drugs in the Anti-Terrorism Campaign," Center for Defense Information, <www.cdi.org/terror ism/narcotics-pr.cfm>, 2 November 2001; from United Nations International Drug Control Programme (UNDCP), *Afghanistan Annual Opium Poppy Survey 2001*, Country Office for Afghanistan, Islamabad, Pakistan, October 2001; from Bertil Lintner and Chiang Mai, "Taliban Turns to Drugs," *Far Eastern Economic Review*, 11 October 2001, pp. 26–27; and from International Crisis Group, *Central Asia: Drugs and Conflict*, ICG Asia Report No. 25, Osh/Brussels, 26 November 2001. **Cambodia** from Michael Ross, "Natural Resources and Civil Conflict: Evidence from Case Studies," University of Michigan, Department of Political Science, 11 May 2001; from Jamie Doward,

"Mineral Riches Fuel War, Not the Poor," *The Observer*, 18 June 2000, and from Global Witness, *The Logs of War. The Timber Trade and Armed Conflict*, published in the series "Economies of Conflict: Private Sector Activity in Armed Conflict," Fafo Institute for Applied Social Science, Programme for International Co-operation and Conflict Resolution, Oslo, Norway, Fafo Report 379, March 2002, pp. 17–21. **Burma** from Global Witness, ibid., pp. 28–31; and from Edith T. Mirante, "Gunboat Petroleum: Burma's Unocal/Total Pipeline," Environmental News Network, 26 April 2002.

5.   Number of conflicts active in 2001 from Arbeitsgemeinschaft Kriegsursachenforschung (AKUF), "Im Schatten des Anti-Terror-Kriegs: Weltweit 46 Kriegerische Konflikte im Jahr 2001," press release (Hamburg, Germany: Institute for Political Science, University of Hamburg), December 2001; one-quarter share of all conflicts having a resource dimension is the author's assessment based on existing literature. Number of deaths derived from data in Milton Leitenberg, "Deaths in Wars and Conflicts Between 1945 and 2000," Center for International and Security Studies, University of Maryland, May 2001 (Paper prepared for Conference on Data Collection in Armed Conflict, Uppsala, Sweden, 8–9 June 2001). Refugee numbers derived from UN High Commissioner for Refugees, <www.unhcr.ch>; number of internally-displaced persons derived from U.S. Committee for Refugees,<www.refugees.org>, both viewed 25 August 2002. Table 1 is a Worldwatch compilation based on numerous sources.

6.   Michael T. Klare, *Resource Wars: The New Landscape of Global Conflict* (New York: Metropolitan Books, 2001), pp. 15, 20–21.

7.   For an overview, see Michael Renner, *Fighting for Survival: Environmental Decline, Social Conflicts, and the New Age of Insecurity* (New York: W.W. Norton & Co., 1996). For a theoretical discussion of the connection between environmental scarcity and conflict, see Thomas F. Homer-Dixon, *Environment, Scarcity, and Violence* (Princeton, NJ: Princeton University Press, 1999). A number of individual cases are discussed in Thomas Homer-Dixon and Jessica Blitt, eds., *Ecoviolence: Links Among Environment, Population, and Security* (Lanham, MD: Rowman & Littlefield Publishers, 1998).

8.   Indra de Soysa, "The Resource Curse: Are Civil Wars Driven by Rapacity or Paucity?" in Mats Berdal and David M. Malone, eds., *Greed and Grievance: Economic Agendas in Civil Wars* (Boulder, CO: Lynne Rienner Publishers, 2000), pp. 113–136. Also see Fred Pearce, "Blood Diamonds and Oil," *New Scientist*, 29 June 2002, pp. 36–40, and Philippe Le Billon, "The Political Ecology of War: Natural Resources and Armed Conflicts," *Political Geography*, No. 20 (2001), pp. 561–584.

9.   Paul Collier, *Economic Causes of Civil Conflict and Their Implications for Policy* (Washington, DC: World Bank, 2000), pp. 3, 4; Paul Collier, "Doing Well Out of War: An Economic Perspective," in Berdal and Malone, op. cit. note 8, pp. 93–97.

10.   International Crisis Group, op. cit. note 4.

11.   Switch from superpower patronage to resource exploitation from Mark Duffield, "Globalization, Transborder Trade, and War Economies," in Berdal and Malone, op. cit., note 8, p. 73, and from Richard Dowden, "War, Money and Survival: Rounding Up," <www.onwar.org/warandmoney/index. html>. Alternative revenue streams from Mary Kaldor, *New and Old Wars: Organized Violence in a Global Era* (Stanford, CA: Stanford University Press, 1999), pp. 102–03, and from David Keen, "Incentives and Disincentives for Violence," in Berdal and Malone, op. cit. note 8, pp. 29–31.

12.   De Beers and UN group of experts estimates from United Nations, Security Council, "Report of the Panel of Experts Appointed Pursuant to Security Council Resolution 1306 (2000), Paragraph 19, in Relation to Sierra Leone" (New York: 20 December 2000); higher estimates of share of conflict diamonds from Christine Gordon, "Rebels' Best Friend," *BBC Focus On Africa*, October–December 1999, cited in Ian Smillie, Lansana Gberie, and Ralph Hazleton, *The Heart of the Matter: Sierra Leone, Diamonds and Human Security* (Ottawa, ON, Canada: Partnership Africa Canada, January 2000); from Fatal Transactions Campaign, op. cit. note 3; and from U.S. Government Accounting Office, *Critical Issues Remain in Deterring Conflict Diamond Trade*, GAO-02-678, (Washington, DC: June 2002), p. 7.

13.   U.S. Government Accounting Office, op. cit. note 12, p. 8.

14.   Global Witness, op. cit. note 4, p. 8. The study quotes a report by the British Royal Institute of International Affairs: "Illegal logging takes place when timber is harvested, transported, bought or sold in violation of national laws. The harvesting procedure itself may be illegal, including corrupt means to gain access to forests, extraction without permission or from a protected area, cutting of protected species or extraction of timber in excess of agreed limits. Illegalities may also occur during transport, including illegal processing and export, misdeclaration to customs, and avoidance of taxes and other monies." Conflict timber is often harvested in ways comparable to those described in the quote.

15.   Le Billon, op. cit. note 8.

16.   Logging observation from Global Witness, op. cit. note 4, p. 8.

17.   Le Billon, op. cit. note 8.

18.   Table 2 is adapted from Michael Ross, "How Does Natural Resource Wealth Influence Civil War?," Department of Political Science, University of California at Los Angeles, 6 December 2001 and revised version of 3 July 2002. The 6 December 2001 version of Prof. Ross' paper contained assessments of 13 conflicts, including Cabinda (Angola), West Papua (Indonesia), and Bougainville (Papua New Guinea). In the revised version, these were replaced by assessments of conflicts in Burma, Colombia, and Peru. Table 2 includes

all 16 cases addressed in the two papers. **Note concerning terms:** *Key Characteristics of Conflict*—**Resource looting** signals that opportunities for resource pillage either helped trigger or prolong conflict; **resource battles** refers to the occurrence of fighting in which opposing forces directly battle over control of resource-rich territories; **cooperative plunder** means that nominally opposing forces at times cooperate in exploiting natural resources in an effort to perpetuate the conditions conducive to their illicit activities; **predatory groups** refers to the rise, assisted by resource wealth exploitation, of abusive armed groups that often engage in indiscriminate violence in pursuit of their objectives; **lack of cohesion** refers to the inability of a combatant force's leadership to make its fighters abide by decisions (prolonging conflict in Liberia, but shortening it in Cambodia); **incentive** and **disincentive** indicate whether there is enticement for combatants to adhere to a peace settlement; **repression** signifies that governments resort to human rights violations and other forms of violence to suppress rebellious or secessionist groups in resource-rich areas; **grievances** means that negative social, economic, and environmental effects of resource extraction help trigger violence. *Conflict Initiation*—**Yes** means that resource exploitation played a discernible role in triggering the outbreak of hostilities. **No** signals the absence of such evidence. *Conflict Duration*—**Prolonged** suggests that recourse to resource wealth extended the length of the conflict (by benefiting the weaker side). **Shortened**, on the other hand, implies that the stronger side benefited primarily or exclusively, allowing it to bring the conflict to a quicker termination. **None** signals that resource wealth did not play a role either way. **Unclear** means that the net impact of resource wealth is difficult to ascertain. *Conflict Intensity*—**Yes** means that resource wealth had a discernible impact on conflict intensity, defined as a heightened casualty rate. **No** signals the absence of such evidence. **Mixed** means that there is no clearcut observable trend (because these conflicts feature, at different times, both intense battles over resources and forms of cooperative plunder).

19.   Kaldor, op. cit. note 11, pp. 90, 98–100; Dowden, op. cit. note 11.

20.   David Keen, "Incentives and Disincentives for Violence," in Berdal and Malone, op. cit. note 8, pp. 22, 24, 27; David Keen, "The Economic Functions of Violence in Civil Wars," *Adelphi Paper 320* (Oxford: Oxford University Press for the International Institute for Strategic Studies, 1998); Kaldor, op. cit. note 11, pp. 110–11.

21.   Jeffrey D. Sachs and Andrew M. Warner, "Natural Resource Abundance and Economic Growth," Development Discussion Paper No. 517a, Harvard Institute for International Development, Cambridge, Massachusetts, 1995; Michael Ross, *Extractive Sectors and the Poor*, Oxfam America, October 2001, pp. 7–9.

22.   Ross, op. cit. note 21, pp. 5, 7; de Soysa, op. cit. note 8, pp. 120, 121, 125, 126.

23.   Ross, op. cit. note 21, pp. 5, 7; Le Billon, op. cit. note 8. Figure 1 is derived from the following sources: International Monetary Fund (IMF), *International*

Financial Statistics Yearbook, 1979 and 2000 editions, and idem, *International Financial Statistics* (monthly), various editions. The IMF price indices are on a current dollar basis and were deflated using the World Bank's Manufacturing Unit Value Index (MUV). This is a U.S. dollar-based index of prices of manufactures exported from leading industrial countries (United States, Japan, Germany, France, United Kingdom), weighted proportionately to these countries' exports to developing countries. The resulting values provide a measure of the real purchasing power of commodity prices on the world market. MUV index values from Donald Mitchell, Development Prospects Group, World Bank, e-mail to author, 26 February 2001.

24. Ross, op. cit. note 21, pp. 8, 11, 12. Unlike minerals-dependent states, oil-dependent countries do not have higher inequity levels than states without high commodities dependence, and oil dependence is more indirectly linked to poverty.

25. de Soysa, op. cit. note 8, pp. 120, 121, 125, 126; Le Billon, op. cit. note 8.

26. William Reno, "Shadow States and the Political Economy of Civil Wars," in Berdal and Malone, op. cit. note 8, pp. 45, 46, 56, 57. Zaïre from Michela Wrong, *In the Footsteps of Mr. Kurtz. Living on the Brink of Disaster in Mobutu's Congo* (New York: HarperCollins, 2001).

27. Ross, op. cit. note 21, pp. 13–14; Global Witness, op. cit. note 4, pp. 7, 15.

28. Reno, in Berdal and Malone, op. cit. note 26, pp. 47–53; Smillie et al., op. cit. note 12, p. 15; Le Billon, op. cit. note 8.

29. Kaldor, op. cit. note 11, pp. 92, 93; Alex de Waal, "Contemporary Warfare in Africa," *IDS Bulletin*, vol. 27, no. 3 (1996); Le Billon, op. cit. note 15.

30. Project Underground, "Militarization & Minerals Tour," <www.moles.org/Project_Underground/ mil/intro.html>, viewed 6 July 2001; Kim Richard Nossal, "Bulls to Bears: The Privatization of War in the 1990s," <www.on war.org/warandmoney/index.html>; International Alert, *The Privatization of Security: Framing a Conflict Prevention and Peacebuilding Policy Agenda* (London, May 2001); Chaloka Beyani and Damian Lilly, *Regulating Private Military Companies* (London: International Alert, September 2001).

31. Occidental from Project Underground, "Colombia: Oxy's Relationship With Military Turns Deadly," 30 June 2001, at CorpWatch, <www.corp watch.org/news/2001/0148. html>; Shell from Reno, op. cit. note 26, p. 52; Talisman from Christian Aid, op. cit. note 4; ExxonMobil from "Exxon 'Helped Torture in Indonesia,'" *BBC News Online*, 22 June 2001; Freeport-McMoRan from Abigail Abrash, "The Amungme, Kamoro & Freeport," *Cultural Survival Quarterly*, Spring 2001, p. 40.

32. Ease of use of small arms and other attributes from Michael Renner, *Small Arms, Big Impact: The Next Challenge of Disarmament*, Worldwatch Paper 137

(Washington, DC: Worldwatch Institute, October 1997), pp. 10–12; statistics and estimates from Small Arms Survey, *Small Arms Survey 2002*, op. cit. note 4, pp. 5, 6, 13, 14.

33. Renner, op. cit. note 32, pp. 33, 34; Small Arms Survey, *Small Arms Survey 2001* (New York: Oxford University Press, 2001), pp. 107–08.

34. Coltan has received considerable media attention. See, for instance, Karl Vick, "Vital Ore Funds Congo's War," *Washington Post*, 19 March 2001; Kristi Essick, "Guns, Money and Cell Phones," *The Standard: Intelligence for the Internet Economy*, 11 June 2001, <www.thestandard.com/article/0,1902, 267 84, pp.html>; Blaine Harden, "The Dirt in the New Machine," *New York Times Magazine*, 12 August 2001, pp. 35–39; Dena Montague, "Stolen Goods: Coltan and Conflict in the Democratic Republic of Congo," *SAIS Review*, Winter-Spring 2002, p. 105.

35. Duffield, op. cit. note 11, p. 84.

36. Mamara quote in Barbara Crossette, "Singling Out Sierra Leone, UN Council Sets Gem Ban," *New York Times*, 6 July 2000.

37. Smillie et al., op. cit. note 12, pp. 8, 14; David Keen, "Going to War: How Rational Is It?" <www.onwar.org/warand money/index.html>; Reno, op. cit. note 8, p. 48; International Rescue Committee from Arms Trade Resource Center, "March Update," distributed by e-mail, 7 March 2000; UNDP, *Human Development Report 2001*, op. cit. note 2, Table 1.

38. Events in Sierra Leone are documented and analyzed by Africa Confidential, "Special Reports. Chronology of Sierra Leone: How Diamonds Fuelled the Conflict," <www.africa-confidential.com/special.htm>, viewed 9 September 2001; by Human Rights Watch, "Sierra Leone: Priorities for the International Community," June 2000, at Global Policy Forum, <www.globalpolicy.org/security/issues/ diamond/hrw2.htm>; by Smillie et al., op. cit. note 12, pp. 8, 14, 15; by United Nations, Security Council, "Tenth Report of the Secretary-General on the United Nations Mission in Sierra Leone," 25 June 2001; and by United Nations, Security Council, "Report of the Panel of Experts Appointed Pursuant to Security Council Resolution 1395 (2002), Paragraph 4, in Relation to Liberia," S/2002/2470, 19 April 2002, p. 15.

39. Character of government forces from Keen, op. cit. note 37, and from Kaldor, op. cit. note 11, p. 94.

40. Keen, op. cit. note 37; Keen, op. cit. note 11, pp. 35–36; William Reno, "War and the Failure of Peacekeeping in Sierra Leone," in SIPRI, op. cit. note 4, p. 151.

41. United Nations, op. cit. note 12, "UN Imposes Diamond Ban on Sierra Leone," *Weekly Defense Monitor*, 14 July 2000.

42. Arms supply routes from United Nations, op. cit. note 12; Figure 2 adapted from *Small Arms Survey*, op. cit. note 33, p. 120.

43. United Nations, op. cit. note 12; Smillie et al., op. cit. note 12, pp. 11, 47.

44. Global Witness, *Taylor-Made—The Pivotal Role of Liberia's Forests in Regional Conflict* (London: 2001); Global Witness, "The Role of Liberia's Logging Industry on National and Regional Insecurity," Briefing to the UN Security Council, January 2001, <www.oneworld.org/ globalwitness/press/ gwliberia.htm>; Greenpeace Spain, *Logs of War: The Relationship Between the Timber Sector, Arms Trafficking and the Destruction of the Forests in Liberia* (Madrid: 2001). Destination of timber from Greenpeace, "Forest Destruction Fuels Regional Conflicts: Environmental and Social Impacts of the Liberian Timber Industry, <www.greenpeace.org/saveordelete/reports/liberia.doc>, November 2001. Discrepancy between revenues and government receipts from Global Witness, op. cit. note 4, pp. 23–26. Other sources report higher Liberian timber trade revenues (of $187 million per year). See *Small Arms Survey 2002*, op. cit. note 4 , p. 142.

45. Global Witness, *Taylor-Made*, op. cit. note 44; Greenpeace Spain, op. cit. note 44; Global Witness, op. cit. note 4, pp. 23–26; United Nations, *Report of the Panel of Experts*, op. cit. note 38, p. 33.

46. United Nations, *Report of the Panel of Experts*, pp. 11, 12, 24, 25; Patrick Alley, "Roden für den Krieg," *Der Überblick*, No. 2/2002, p. 59.

47. United Nations Office for the Coordination of Humanitarian Affairs, "Sierra Leone: Conflict in Liberia Poses Threat to Stability—Annan," *IRIN News* (Integrated Regional Information Networks), 26 June 2002. Annan's full report is available at the United Nations' Web site, <www.un.org/Docs/ sc/reports/2002/sgrep02.htm>.

48. Montague, op. cit. note 34, pp. 106–110; Ross, op. cit. note 18; Robert Block, "As Zaire's War Wages, Foreign Businesses Scramble for Inroads," *Wall Street Journal*, 14 April 1997. For a discussion of the wealth grab during Belgium's colonial rule, see the gripping account by Adam Hochschild, *King Leopold's Ghost: A Story of Greed, Terror, and Heroism in Colonial Africa* (New York: Houghton Mifflin, 1999).

49. Estimates of deaths reported in Norimitsu Onishi, "African Numbers, Problems and Number Problems," *New York Times*, 18 August 2002; displacements from Taylor B. Seybolt, "Major Armed Conflicts," in SIPRI, op. cit. note 4, p. 26; foreign troops from "Peace Here Means War Elsewhere," *The Economist*, 23 June 2001, p. 44; Colette Braeckman, "Congo: A War Without Victors," *Le Monde Diplomatique*, English Language Edition, April 2001. Uganda and Rwanda initially supported the Rassemblement Congolais pour la Democratie (RCD), formed in August 1998. But as tensions increased between the two countries and led to fighting in 1999 and 2000, they backed different factions, respectively RCD-ML and RCD-Goma. As the Congo conflict has worn on, the different rebel forces have increasingly splintered, with shifting alliances forming. See Christian Dietrich, *Hard Currency: The Criminalized Diamond Economy of the Democratic Republic of the Congo and Its Neighbors*, The Diamonds and Human Security Project, Occasional Paper No. 4, Ottawa, Canada, June 2002, pp. 39, 40.

50.   United Nations, Security Council, "Report of the Panel of Experts on the Illegal Exploitation of Natural Resources and Other Forms of Wealth of the Democratic Republic of the Congo" (New York: 12 April 2001), pp. 41, 42. Figure 3 adapted from Philippe Rekacewicz, *Le Monde Diplomatique*, Paris, July 2000.

51.   Ibid., pp. 11, 14; United Nations, Security Council, "Addendum to the Report of the Panel of Experts on the Illegal Exploitation of Natural Resources and Other Forms of Wealth of the Democratic Republic of the Congo," 13 November 2001; Harden, op. cit. note 34, pp. 37–38; Musifiky Mwanalasi, "The View From Below," in Berdal and Malone, op. cit. note 8, p. 142; International Peace Information Service, *Supporting the War Economy in the DRC: European Companies and the Coltan Trade*, Antwerp, Belgium, January 2002.

52.   United Nations, op. cit. note 50, pp. 3, 7, 14–19, 29–31; United Nations, op. cit. note 51, p. 20; Vick, op. cit. note 34. Kagame quote from Montague, op. cit. note 34, p. 112.

53.   Emasculation of state mining companies from Wrong, op. cit. note 26, pp. 113–118, 122–125; United Nations, op. cit. note 51, pp. 5, 8, 9. Monthly diamond revenues from Andrew Cockburn, "Diamonds: The Real Story," *National Geographic*, March 2002, p. 22.

54.   Ross, op. cit. note 18; United Nations, op. cit. note 50, pp. 29–36; Vick, op. cit. note 34. Zimbabwe's economic difficulties from Michael Nest, "Ambitions, Profits and Loss: Zimbabwean Economic Involvement in the Democratic Republic of the Congo," *African Affairs*, no. 400 (2001), pp. 469–490, and from Dietrich, op. cit. note 49, pp. 41–42.

55.   United Nations, op. cit. note 51, pp. 10–11, 16–19, 22; Nest, op. cit. note 54. Timber concession from Global Witness, op. cit. note 4, pp. 35–37. Ridgepoint from Reno, op. cit. note 26, pp. 57–58.

56.   United Nations, op. cit. note 51, pp. 10, 11, 16–18, 22.

57.   United Nations, op. cit. note 50, pp. 37–39; "Sabena/Swissair Declares Embargo on Transport of Coltan," *Africa News*, 21 June 2001.

58.   Henri E. Cauvin, "Rwanda and Congo Sign Accord to End War," *New York Times*, 31 July 2002; Marc Lacey, "Congo Peace Accord Evokes Cautious Hope," *New York Times*, 6 August 2002; Makau Mutua, "Struggling to End Africa's World War" (op-ed), *New York Times*, 2 August 2002; UN Office for the Coordination of Humanitarian Affairs, "DRC-Uganda: Kampala to Withdraw

Troops, Bilateral Relations to be Normalized," *IRIN News*, 18 August 2002.

59. Global Witness, *A Rough Trade: The Role of Companies and Governments in the Angolan Conflict* (London: 1998). Cease-fire from Rachel L. Swarns, "Angolans Cheer the Peace and Hope It Will Stay Awhile," *New York Times*, 5 April 2002.

60. Virginia Gamba and Richard Cornwell, "Arms, Elites, and Resources in the Angolan Civil War," in Berdal and Malone, op. cit. note 8, pp. 165–67; diamond production from Smillie, op. cit. note 12; oil production from BP Amoco, *2001 BP Amoco Statistical Review of World Energy* (London: Group Media & Publications, 2001).

61. Trends in UNITA diamond income from Global Witness, op. cit. note 59; from Harden, op. cit. note 34; and from Ross, op. cit. note 4; use of diamond income from United Nations, Security Council, "Final Report of the UN Panel of Experts on Violations of Security Council Sanctions Against Unita" (New York: 10 March 2000).

62. United Nations, op. cit. note 61; Global Witness, op. cit. note 59. Number of 100,000 diggers from Cockburn, op. cit. note 53, p. 23.

63. De Beers decision to stop buying Angolan diamonds from United Nations, op. cit. note 61; Global Witness, op. cit. note 59; Duffield, op. cit. note 11, p. 84.

64. Smuggling routes from United Nations, op. cit. note 12, and from Global Witness, op. cit. note 59; polishing in Israel and Ukraine from Gamba and Cornwell, op. cit. note 60, p. 166.

65. United Nations, op. cit. note 61; Figure 4 from Small Arms Survey, op. cit. note 33, p. 116.

66. Doward, op. cit. note 4; Global Witness, op. cit. note 2, pp. 4, 6, 7; Ross, op. cit. note 18.

67. Global Witness, op. cit. note 2, pp. 5–7, 11, 12.

68. Ibid., pp. 7, 13–16.

69. Jason Mark, "Colombia: Washington's Next Dirty War," *Global Exchange Newsletter,* 1 June 2000, at <www.globalexchange.org/Colombia/dirtywar.html>, viewed 24 April 2002; Juan Ferero, "New Colombian President Gets Jump Start on Country's Problems," *New York Times*, 7 August 2002; María Cristina Caballero, "Is Colombia Doomed to Repeat Its Past?," *New York Times*, 10 August 2002. Figure 5 based on the map "Colombian Overdose," by Nigel Holmes/*Harper's Magazine*, February 2002.

70. Mark, op. cit. note 69; U.S. Department of State, Bureau of Western Hemisphere Affairs, "Background Note: Colombia," April 2002,

<www.state.gov/r/pa/ei/bgn/1831.htm>, viewed 24 April 2002. FARC and ELN fighters from Washington Office on Latin America, "Plan Colombia: U.S. Military Aid Fueling Brutal Civil War," at <www.wola.org>, viewed 24 April 2002, pp. 4–5; AUC from "A Call to Arms," *The Economist*, 28 February 2002, at <www.economist.com/PrinterFriendly.cfm?Story_ID=1011247>, viewed 5 April 2002.

71.   Washington Office on Latin America, op. cit. note 70, p. 5; Lynn Holland, "Shades of Gray," (Silver City, NM: Interhemispheric Resource Center, 1 March 2002) <www.americaspolicy.org/commentary/2002/body_0203colombia.html>; Gina Amatangelo, "Militarization of the U.S. Drug Control Program," *Foreign Policy In Focus*, vol. 6, no. 17, May 2001; U.S. General Accounting Office, "Drug Control: Challenges in Implementing Plan Colombia," Statement of Jess T. Ford, Director International Affairs and Trade, 12 October 2000, Testimony Before the Subcommittee on Criminal Justice, Drug Policy, and Human Resources, Committee on Government Reform, House of Representatives, p. 5. FARC annual earnings from Small Arms Survey, op. cit. note 32, p. 142.

72.   U.S. Department of State, op. cit. note 70; Karl Penhaul, "Along the Pipeline: Tracking Colombia's Revolt,", *Boston Globe*, 21 April 2002; Martin Hodgson, "Oil Inflames Colombia's Civil War," *Christian Science Monitor*, 4 March 2002.

73.   Steven Dudley, "War in Colombia's Oilfields," *The Nation*, 5/12 August 2002, pp. 28–31; Thad Dunning and Leslie Wirpsa, "Oil Rigged," Resource Center of the Americas, February 2001, as posted at Global Policy Forum, <www.globalpolicy.org/security/natres/oil/2001/0201colo.htm>; Project Underground, "Colombia: Oxy's Relationship with Military Turns Deadly," 30 June 2001, as posted at CorpWatch, <www.corpwatch.org/news/201/0148.html>; Hodgson, op. cit. note 72; Andrew Selsky, "US Plans for Wider Colombia Involvement. Goal of Aid Plan is Protecting Oil," *Boston Globe*, 6 February 2002; Rainforest Action Network, "In Defense of Sacred Lands: The U'wa People's Struggle Against Big Oil," <www.ran.org/ran_campaigns/beyond_oil/oxy/uwa_facts.html> viewed 24 July 2002.

74.   War tax from Dunning and Wirpsa, op. cit. note 73; Project Underground, op. cit. note 73. U.S. aid from Nina M. Serafino, "Colombia: Summary and Tables on U.S. Assistance, FY1989-FY2003," Congressional Research Service, Library of Congress, Washington, DC, 3 May 2002; from Washington Office on Latin America, op. cit. note 70, p. 1; and from "Fighting for Colombian Oil," *San Francisco Chronicle*, 13 February 2002.

75.   Ibon Villelabeitia, "Colombian U'wa Indians Brace for New Battle," *Reuters*, 9 July 2002; Rainforest Action Network, op. cit. note 73.

76.   Villelabeitia, op. cit. note 75; Rainforest Action Network, op. cit. note 73.

77.   U'wa Defense Working Group, "Occidental Petroleum to Leave U'wa Land! Company Announces Plans to Leave Controversial Colombia Oil Project," Press

Release, 6 May 2002, <www.ran.org/news/newsitem.php?id=531&area=oil>.

78. International Crisis Group, *Indonesia: Natural Resources and Law Enforcement*, ICG Asia Report No. 29, Jakarta and Brussels, 20 December 2001, pp. 10, 18.

79. "Aceh: Ecological War Zone," *Down to Earth*, November 2000; "Exxon's Aceh Plant Shutdowns to Affect Oil and Gas Delivery in Asia," press release, *Far Eastern Economic Review Online*, 21 March 2001; "Exxon 'Helped Torture in Indonesia,'" *BBC News Online*, 22 June 2001; "Activists Set Sights on Exxon-Mobil for 'Complicity of Silence,'" <www.corpwatch.org>, 7 June 2001; John McBeth, "Too Hot to Handle," *Far Eastern Economic Review Online*, 29 March 2001; Ross, op. cit. note 4, pp. 24, 25; International Crisis Group, *Aceh: Can Autonomy Stem the Conflict?*, ICG Asia Report No. 18 (Brussels: 27 June 2001), p. 5.

80. Human Rights Watch, "Indonesia: Why Aceh Is Exploding," press backgrounder (New York: August 1999); "Aceh: Ecological War Zone," *Down to Earth*, op. cit. note 79.

81. Human Rights Watch, op. cit. note 80; International Crisis Group, op. cit. note 79, p. 3; Ross, op. cit. note 4, pp. 23–26; Dini Djalal, "Silencing the Voices of Aceh," *Far Eastern Economic Review Online*, 5 July 2001; Jane Perlez, "A Long War Slices Deep in Indonesia," *New York Times*, 17 June 2002; Jane Perlez, "Indonesia's Guerrilla War Puts Exxon Under Siege," *New York Times*, 14 July 2002; Dan Murphy, "Military Reasserts Power, Casualties Mount in Aceh," *Christian Science Monitor*, 24 July 2002. Death toll in 2001 from Jane Perlez, "Visiting Indonesia, U.S. Envoy Seeks to End Rebel Conflict," *New York Times*, 9 August 2002, and earlier years from Seybolt, op. cit. note 49, p. 38.

82. McBeth, op. cit. note 79; "Exxon's Aceh Plant Shutdowns to Affect Oil and Gas Delivery in Asia," op. cit. note 79; Wayne Arnold, "ExxonMobil, in Fear, Exits Indonesian Gas Fields," *New York Times*, 24 March 2001; "Violence Spirals in Troubled Aceh," *BBC News Online*, 18 March 2001; "Exxon Back on Stream in Indonesia," BBC News Online, 19 July 2001; new counterinsurgency operation from Sidney Jones, "For Indonesia, A Sea of Troubles" (op-ed), *New York Times*, 27 July 2001.

83. Robert Jereski, "Activist and Press Backgrounder on ExxonMobil Activities in North Aceh," International Forum for Aceh, 27 May 2001, viewed at East Timor Action Network, <www.etan.org>, 24 July 2001; "Mobil Oil and Human Rights Abuse in Aceh," *Down to Earth*, November 1998; "Exxon 'Helped Torture in Indonesia,'" *BBC News Online*, 22 June 2001; "Exxon Mobil-Sponsored Terrorism?," *The Nation*, 14 June 2002; Perlez, op. cit. note 81; Jane Perlez, "U.S. Backs Oil Giant on Lawsuit in Indonesia," *New York Times*, 8 August 2002.

84. Ross, op. cit. note 4, p. 27; "No Flags for Papua," *The Economist*, 12 October 2000; Human Rights Watch, *Violence and Political Impasse in Papua* (New York: July 2001), p. 2.

85. "Risky Business: The Grasberg Gold Mine," Project Underground Reports, <www. moles.org/index.htm>, viewed 9 July 2001; "The Strains on Indonesia," *The Economist*, 3 December 2000; "Provocation," *The Economist*, 30 November 2000; Abrash, op. cit. note 31, pp. 38–39; Michael Shari, "Freeport-McMoRan—A Pit of Trouble," *Business Week*, 31 July 2000.

86. Ross, op. cit. note 4, p. 28; Javanese immigration and disproportionate division of benefits from Human Rights Watch, op. cit. note 84, p. 19; *Rape and Other Human Rights Abuses by the Indonesian Military in Irian Jaya (West Papua), Indonesia* (Washington, DC: Robert F. Kennedy Memorial Center for Human Rights, May 1999); Abrash, op. cit. note 31, p. 40.

87. Human Rights Watch, op. cit. note 84, pp. 2, 3, 10, 11; Jim Lobe, "Indonesia's Hard Line Strengthens Secessionists in West Papua," *Foreign Policy in Focus*, 1 July 2001.

88. "Talking About a Devolution," *The Economist*, 4 January 2000; "Megawati Sorry for Rights Abuses," BBC News Online, 16 August 2001; autonomy bill from Jim Lobe, "Indonesia: Aceh Arrests Could Portend Increased Polarization, Violence," *Foreign Policy in Focus*, 1 July 2001.

89. Klare, op. cit. note 6, p. 196; "Chronology," *Accord*, No. 12/2002, special issue on "Weaving Consensus: The Papua New Guinea-Bougainville Peace Process," <www.c-r.org/accord/accord12/chron.htm>.

90. Mary-Louise O'Callaghan, "The Origins of the Conflict," *Accord*, op. cit. note 89. Annual revenues from Klare, op. cit. note 6. Environmental damage from Volker Böge, "Bougainville: A 'Classical' Environmental Conflict?," Occasional Paper No. 3, Environment and Conflicts Project (ENCOP), Bern, Switzerland, October 1992.

91. O'Callaghan, op. cit. note 90.

92. "Chronology," *Accord*, op. cit. note 89; $36 million figure from Klare, op. cit. note 6, p. 198.

93. "Chronology," *Accord*, op. cit. note 89; Robert Tapi, "From Burnham to Buin: Sowing the Seeds of Peace in the Land of the Snow-Capped Mountains," *Accord*, op. cit. note 89; "Papua New Guinea: Security Council Members Back Peace Plan," *UN Wire*, 15 August 2001; "Autonomy Approved for Bougainville," *UN Wire*, 28 March 2002.

94. Renner, op. cit. note 7, pp. 57–58; Human Rights Watch, *The Price of Oil: Corporate Responsibility and Human Rights Violations in Nigeria's Oil Producing Communities* (New York: January 1999); Global Exchange and Essential Action, *Oil for Nothing: Multinational Corporations, Environmental Destruction, Death and Impunity in the Niger Delta* (San Francisco, CA, and Washington, DC: January 2000); Marina Ottaway, "Reluctant Missionaries," *Foreign Policy*, July/August 2001, p. 48.

95. Human Rights Watch, op. cit. note 94; Renner, op. cit. note 7, pp. 57–58.

96. Human Rights Watch, op. cit. note 94; Global Exchange and Essential Action, op. cit. note 94; Shell from Reno, op. cit. note 26, p. 52.

97. Human Rights Watch, op. cit. note 94; Human Rights Commission from Global Exchange and Essential Action, op. cit. note 94, from Chris Simpson, "Shell Overtures to Ogonis," *BBC News Online*, 25 July 2001, and from Barnaby Phillips, "No End to Saro-Wiwa's Struggle," *BBC News Online*, 15 January 2001. "Tragedy in the Nigerian Delta," *New York Times*, 13 June 2002; Jim Lobe, "People versus Big Oil: Rights of Nigerian Indigenous People Recognized," Self-Determination News, Foreign Policy-in-Focus, <www.selfdetermine.org/news/0207nigeria_body.html>, 5 July 2002. One of the protests that was picked up widely in Western media was a peaceful blockade by 150 women of a ChevronTexaco oil export terminal, demanding that the company pay for local schools, electricity, and water. D'arcy Doran, "Nigerian Village Women Agree to End Siege of ChevronTexaco Oil Terminal," *Associated Press*, 16 July 2002.

98. Global intact forest area assessment from UN Environment Programme, *An Assessment of the Status of the World's Remaining Closed Forests* (Nairobi: 2001); Congo birds, mammals, and wealth of flora from Terese Hart and Robert Mwinyihali, *Armed Conflict and Biodiversity in Sub-Saharan Africa: The Case of the Democratic Republic of Congo (DRC)* (Washington, DC: Biodiversity Support Program, 2001), p. 12; forest loss in 1990s from "Forests: Deforestation Continuing Worldwide at High Rate, FAO Warns," *UN Wire*, 3 October 2001. The UN Food and Agriculture Organization found in its *State of the World's Forests 2001* assessment that the countries with the highest net loss of forest area between 1990 and 2000 were Argentina, Brazil, the Democratic Republic of the Congo, Indonesia, Mexico, Myanmar, Nigeria, Sudan, Zambia, and Zimbabwe.

99. For an overview, see John E. Young, *Discarding the Throwaway Society*, Worldwatch Paper 101 (Washington, DC: January 1991), pp. 7–12; Janet N. Abramovitz, *Taking a Stand: Cultivating a New Relationship with the World's Forests*, Worldwatch Paper 140 (Washington, DC: April 1998), pp. 22–38; and Gary Gardner and Payal Sampat, *Mind Over Matter: Recasting the Role of Materials in Our Lives*, Worldwatch Paper 144 (Washington, DC: December 1998), pp. 17–20.

100. Klare, op. cit. note 6, pp. 203–07; percent of loggers following ecological guidelines from Janis B. Alcorn, "An Introduction to the Linkages between Ecological Resilience and Governance," in Janis B. Alcorn and Antoinette G. Royo, eds., *Indigenous Social Movements and Ecological Resilience: Lessons from the Dayak of Indonesia* (Washington, DC: Biodiversity Support Program, 2000), p. 10.

101. Stefanus Masiun, "National Frameworks Affecting *Adat* Governance in

Indonesia, and Dayak NGO Responses," in Alcorn and Royo, op. cit. note 100, pp. 23–24; Robin Broad, "The Political Economy of Natural Resources: Case Studies of the Indonesian and Philippine Forest Sectors," *The Journal of Developing Areas*, April 1995, pp. 322–26.

102. John Bamba, "Land, Rivers, and Forests: Dayak Solidarity and Ecological Resilience," in Alcorn and Royo, op. cit. note 100, pp. 46–48. Central Kalimantan from International Crisis Group, op. cit. note 78, pp. 3–4. Area still forested from Alcorn, op. cit. note 100, p. 8. West Kalimantan from Bamba, op. cit. this note, and from Masiun, op. cit. note 101, p. 24.

103. Biodiversity of central Borneo and Dayak way of life from Alcorn, op. cit. note 100, pp. 6, 9. Dan Murphy, "Behind Ethnic War, Indonesia's Old Migration Policy," *Christian Science Monitor*, 1 March 2001; Broad, op. cit. note 101, pp. 322–26; International Crisis Group, op. cit. note 78, pp. 3, 4.

104. This juxtaposition of the immediate cash-in value of resources versus the long-term preservation of biodiversity is made by Hart and Mwinyihali, op. cit. note 98, p. 12.

105. José Kalpers, *Volcanoes Under Siege: Impact of a Decade of Armed Conflict in the Virungas* (Washington, DC: Biodiversity Support Program, 2001).

106. Hart and Mwinyihali, op. cit. note 98, pp. 14, 19, 21, 25.

107. UNESCO, "The World Heritage List," <www.unesco.org/whc/heritage.ht m#debut>, and "World Heritage List in Danger," <www.unesco.org/whc/dan glist.htm>, both viewed 11 August 2001; United Nations, op. cit. note 50, pp. 10–12; "Miners' Rush for Coltan Threatens Rare Gorilla," *Environment News Service,* 13 April 2001; "One Minute to Midnight for Great Apes," *The Ecologist,* July/August 2001, p. 15; Harden, op. cit. note 34.

108. United Nations, op. cit. note 50, pp. 10–12.

109. Chris Squire, *Sierra Leone's Biodiversity and the Civil War* (Washington, DC: Biodiversity Support Program, 2001).

110. Greenpeace Spain, op. cit. note 44; Global Witness, *Taylor-Made,* op. cit. note 44; Global Witness, *The Logs of War,* op. cit. note 44, p. 27.

111. Table 4 compiled from United Nations, Security Council Documents Full Search, <www.un.org/Docs/sc>, from United Nations, op. cit. note 12, and from United Nations, op. cit. note 50, pp. 41–45; France and China from Global Witness, *Taylor-Made,* op. cit. note 44, p. 6.

112. Human Rights Watch, "Neglected Arms Embargo on Sierra Leone Rebels," Briefing Paper, 15 May 2000, as posted on Global Policy Forum, <www.glob alpolicy.org/security/issues/sierra/00-05sl4.htm>; United Nations, op. cit. note 12.

113. Alan Cowell, "New 'Labels' for Diamonds Sold by Sierra Leone," *New York Times*, 28 October 2000; United Nations, op. cit. note 38, pp. 26, 28–29. Diamond fingerprinting technology from Smillie et al., op. cit. note 12, pp. 63–64.

114. "Angola: Diamonds Worth $1 Million Smuggled Daily, UN Says," *UN Wire*, 16 October 2001; Norimitsu Onishi, "Africa Diamond Hub Defies Smuggling Rules," *New York Times*, 2 January 2001; Andrew Parker, "Checks 'May Not Halt All Illicit Diamond Exports,'" *Financial Times*, 25 April 2001; Global Witness, op. cit. note 59; United Nations, op. cit. note 12; idem, op. cit. note 61.

115. Judy Dempsey and Andrew Parker, "Belgium, UK in Drive to Halt War Gems," *Financial Times*, 26 June 2001. Efforts by Belgium and Diamond High Council from United Nations, op. cit. note 51, p. 11; from Partnership Africa Canada, "Human Security and the International Diamond Trade in Africa," <www.partnershipafricacanada.org/hsdp/index.html>, viewed 11 June 2002, and from UN Office for the Coordination of Humanitarian Affairs, "DRC-Rwanda-Uganda: Mandate of UN Expert Panel on Resource Exploitation Extended," *IRIN News*, 19 July 2002. U.S. efforts from Ken Silverstein, "Diamonds of Death," *The Nation*, 23 April 2001, pp. 19–20; from Campaign to Eliminate Conflict Diamonds, "Questions and Answers About Conflict Diamonds and the 'Clean Diamonds Act,'" <www.phrusa.org/campaigns/sierra_leone/diam_q&a. html>, viewed 10 September 2001; and from Oxfam America, "Conflict Diamonds Drive Wars in Africa," <www.oxfamamerica.org/advocacy/art826.html>.

116. Ken Silverstein, op. cit. note 115, p. 20; "Diamonds: EU to Discuss Conflict Gems; US Senators Propose Ban," *UN Wire*, 26 June 2001; Campaign to Eliminate Conflict Diamonds, "Governments and Industry: Stop Blood Diamonds Now!" 21 August 2001, <www.phrusa.org/campaigns/sierra_leone/jewel_release082101.html>; "Diamonds: Kimberley Process Reaches Breakthrough on Certification," *UN Wire*, 22 March 2002.

117. Ian Smillie, "Conflict Diamonds: Unfinished Business," International Development Research Centre, <www.idrc.ca/media/Conflict_Diamonds_e.html>, 27 May 2002.

118. U.S. Government Accounting Office, op. cit. note 12, pp. 17–21.

119. Lack of international rules and UNFF from Global Witness, op. cit. note 4, pp. 48, 52. Forest Stewardship Council from Gary Gereffi, Ronie Garcia-Johnson, and Erika Sasser, "The NGO-Industrial Complex," *Foreign Policy*, July/August 2001, pp. 60–61; United Nations, op. cit. note 50, pp. 41–45.

120. In the mid-1990s, for example, human rights and environmental organizations launched campaigns aimed at Shell (for its role in Nigeria) and at Amoco, Texaco, ARCO, and Petro-Canada (for their roles in Myanmar); Ottaway, op. cit. note 94, pp. 47–48.

121. Harden, op. cit. note 34; Nicole Gaouette, "Israel's Diamond Dealers Tremble," *Christian Science Monitor*, 1 June 2001; Smillie et al. op. cit. note 12, p. 9; electronics companies' reaction from Harden, op. cit. note 34, p. 38, and from Essick, op. cit. note 34; Kemet and Cabot from United Nations, op. cit. note 51, p. 6; Talisman from Dena Montague, "U.S. Debates Sudanese Oil and Peace," Arms Trade Resource Center Update, World Policy Institute, New York, 27 June 2002, available electronically at <www.worldpolicy.org/projects/arms>.

122. United Nations, op. cit. note 51, pp. 7, 15; International Labor Rights Fund, "ExxonMobil: Genocide, Murder and Torture in Aceh, Indonesia," <www.laborrights.org/projects/corporate/exxon/index.html>, viewed 16 July 16, 2002.

123. David Corn, "Corporate Human Rights," *The Nation*, 15 July 2002, p. 31; "Oily Diplomacy," *New York Times*, 19 August 2002.

124. The coalition includes, among others, Amnesty International, Christian Aid, Friends of the Earth, Global Witness, Oxfam, Save the Children, and Transparency International. George Soros, "Transparent Corruption," *Financial Times*, 13 June 2002; Transparency International, "Press Release: George Soros and NGOs Call for Rules to Require Corporations to Disclose Payments," <www.transparency.org/pressreleases_archive/2002/2002.06.13.publish_pay.ht ml>, viewed 25 June 2002.

125. "Hotspots!" *New Internationalist*, June 2001, pp. 22–23; Norimitsu Onishi with Neela Banerjee, "Chad's Wait for Its Oil Riches May Be Long," *New York Times*, 16 May 2001; Abid Aslam and Jim Lobe, "Bush-Cheney Energy Plan Could Aggravate Ethnic Conflicts," Crisis Watch, *Foreign Policy in Focus*, <www.fpif.org/selfdetermination/crisiswatch/energy_body.html>, viewed 3 August 2001.

126. Association Tchadienne pour la Promotion et la Défense des Droits de l'Homme (Chad), Centre pour l'Environnement et le Developpement (Cameroon), and Environmental Defense (USA), *The Chad-Cameroon Oil and Pipeline Project: A Call for Accountability* (N'Djamena, Chad, Yaounde, Cameroon, and Washington, DC: June 2002); UN Office for the Coordination of Humanitarian Affairs, "Cameroon-Chad: Oil-Pipeline Risks Cry Out for Action—NGOs," *IRIN News*, 8 August 2002; "Chad-Cameroon: World Bank Panel Criticizes Bank-Backed Pipeline Project," *UN Wire*, 19 August 2002, <www.unwire.org/unwire/2002/08/19/current.asp#28414>.

127. Hilary French, "Socially Responsible Investing Surges," in Worldwatch Institute, *Vital Signs 2001* (New York: W.W. Norton & Company, 2001), pp. 114–15

128. *Small Arms Survey 2001*, op. cit. note 33, pp. 251–83; the Declaration of a Moratorium on the Importation, Exportation and Manufacture of Small Arms and Light Weapons in West Africa was adopted by the members of Economic Community of West African States; see United Nations, op. cit. note 12;

United Nations, op. cit. note 38, p. 16.

129. Rachel Stohl, "United States Weakens Outcome of UN Small Arms and Light Weapons Conference," *Arms Control Today,* September 2001.

130. Rachel L. Swarns, "Congo and Rwanda Reach Tentative Peace Pact," *New York Times,* 23 July 2002. Under the agreement, the Rwandan government promised to withdraw its forces from the Congo in return from a pledge by the Congolese government that it would stop harboring Rwandan guerrilla forces that have conducted raids into Rwanda since the mid-1990s.

131. Michael Renner, "UN Peacekeeping: An Uncertain Future," *Foreign Policy in Focus,* September 2000; Michael Renner, "Peacekeeping Expenditures Rebound," in Worldwatch Institute, op. cit. note 127, pp. 84–85.

Index

Other Worldwatch Papers

Other Publications From the Worldwatch Institute

State of the World 2003   Coming Soon!
Worldwatch's flagship annual is used by government officials, corporate planners, journalists, development specialists, professors, students, and concerned citizens in over 120 countries. Published in more than 20 different languages, it is one of the most widely used resources for analysis.

State of the World Library 2002
Subscribe to the *State of the World Library* and join thousands of decisionmakers and concerned citizens who stay current on emerging environmental issues. The *State of the World Library* includes Worldwatch's flagship annual, *State of the World*, plus all five of the highly readable, up-to-date, and authoritative *Worldwatch Papers* as they are published throughout the calendar year.

Signposts 2002
This CD-ROM provides instant, searchable access to over 965 pages of full text from the last two editions of *State of the World* and *Vital Signs*, comprehensive data sets going back as far as 50 years, and easy-to-understand graphs and tables. Fully indexed, *Signposts 2002* contains a powerful search engine for effortless search and retrieval. Plus, it is platform independent and fully compatible with all Windows (3.1 and up), Macintosh, and Unix/Linux operating systems.

Vital Signs 2002
Written by Worldwatch's team of researchers, this annual provides comprehensive, user-friendly information on key trends and includes tables and graphs that help readers assess the developments that are changing their lives for better or for worse.

World Watch
This award-winning bimonthly magazine is internationally recognized for the clarity and comprehensiveness of its articles on global trends. Keep up to speed on the latest developments in population growth, climate change, species extinction, and the rise of new forms of human behavior and governance.

To make a tax-deductible contribution or to order any of Worldwatch's publications, call us toll-free at 888-544-2303 (or 570-320-2076 outside the U.S.), fax us at 570-322-2063, e-mail us at wwpub@worldwatch.org or visit our website at www.worldwatch.org.